TESTIMON

I love the way Steve naturally and calmly inspires! The simplicity of the insight that he shares is key and I am sure that is why it is so successful.

Lee Etheridge, BareMinerals

The "Spiral of Positivity" is a great tool to enable our staff across the whole Trust to understand that they choose how they respond to whatever happens to them during the day and it is no surprise that it has become the signature for the programme. We would recommend Energize to any organisation that truly wishes to help its front-line teams at any level engage positively with their customers, the patients, using a straight forward method.

Maxine Foster, Chelsea & Westminster Hospital

Steve's "Living Our Customers First" sales training has generated a service step change within the business. We would certainly recommend Energize to other organisations and fully intend to take advantage of his other programmes.

Andrew Crooks, Marks and Spencer

I congratulate Steve for the excellent training programme he designed and delivered for our premier clubs. The feedback has been extremely positive with many comments of "What a refreshing approach to training" especially from the clubs who have carried out plenty of training in the past. We are looking forward to rolling these principles out further across the clubs to the other areas where staff interact with the fans – and to working with him on further programmes in the future.

Cathy Long, The Premier League

FIRED UP AND READY TO GO!

Developing life-changing skills to benefit you and your customer

Steven Harris

2000

First published in 2015 by Management Books 2000 Ltd
36 Western Road
Oxford OX1 4LG
Tel: 0044 (0) 1865 600738
Email: info@mb2000.com
Web: www.mb2000.com

British Library Cataloguing in Publication Data is available

ISBN 9781852527600

CONTENTS

ACKNOWLEDGEMENTS

Thank you for choosing to read this book. I really hope you enjoy it and that you feel there is something contained within it for you and for all members of your organisation either who directly engage with customers or those that support those that do in your central support offices.

If you have any questions, comments or stories of your own about good or bad customer service I would love to hear about them. Please feel free to email them to info@energizelearning.com.

If you would like me to come and talk to you, work with you or present at one of your meetings or conferences I would be delighted to do so. You can email me direct at steve@energizelearning.com.

I would like to thank everyone for their encouragement and genuine excitement when they found out I was writing this book. I would also like to thank all my clients who have embraced and implemented many of the principles I have shared with you. I am grateful for their continued support.

In particular I would like to thank the following people:

Richard Wolff and David Brown for agreeing to write the forewords to this book. They have been great mentors and supporters of the work we do at Energize since its inception as well as a good friends. Annabel Wright, Arjan Schimmel and Kevin Waters whose help writing this has been invaluable. James Essinger, my editor, and Nick Dale-Harris and his team at Management Books 2000.

Finally, I would like to thank my family for their constant support. Alex and Tori whose very existence has taught me to love the art of difference and my wife Kathryn for reading and re-reading this book as it has developed but most importantly for being my soul mate for the last 27 years.

I really hope *Fired up and Ready to Go!* helps to support you achieve all the things you want in your life and inspires you to take the next steps towards achieving them.

Thank you!

ABOUT THE AUTHOR

Steven Harris has many years' experience in the fields of customer and employee engagement. He is passionate about helping organisations drive a customer-centric culture. As a practitioner as well as a thought leader, his conferences and workshops focus on real people in the real world. He has appeared on the Richard and Judy show on British television and he presents at many retail, healthcare, leisure and public sector conferences both within the UK, across Europe and in the USA.

Steven has a particular interest in the relationship between our feelings and our performance. He firmly believes that the better we feel, the better we perform.

In 1999, Steven founded Energize Learning, now an award-winning training consultancy which over the last 16 years has worked with over 100 different organisations and reached over 85,000 people.

Before setting up Energize, he spent 20 years working in retail operations, buying and merchandising and franchising, during which time he held several commercial management positions within the major retailer Marks and Spencer, culminating in a two-year appointment at their prestigious flagship store Marble Arch in London. He then joined The Body Shop, rising through the ranks from Area Manager to Head of Retail for both Company-owned and Franchise stores.

Steven has a personal interest in self-esteem and motivation within the education sector and as a London Education Authority Governor he has worked directly with groups of schoolchildren and has run workshops aimed at helping to build self-confidence. He has also spent time advising an American education business, Sylvan Learning, which helps to build confidence in school age children's numeracy and literacy through computer-based learning.

FOREWORDS

I am delighted to pen some words by way of foreword for Steve's excellent book.

Steve and I have known each other for around fifteen years, meeting at Marks and Spencer when he taught the readily understandable Energize's spiral concept to our UK store teams. In later years I asked him to extend his work to our UK Retail Outlet team and also our Marks and Spencer International Partners. Therefore becoming used across many parts of the world. When it comes to employee motivation I cannot think of a better qualified person than Steve which is demonstrated by his impressive client list. I am very pleased for everyone that he has now put his thoughts and techniques into a book. It deserves to do well!

A few words on the way that Steve makes learning fun and relevant. I used to top and tail the groups both in the UK and around the world. They would at first be a little nervous. In no time they would enjoy the storytelling and understand the role that they could play in building relationships with their customers. They would move on to see what fun this could be. The most interesting thing for me would be to see them at the end of the sessions. They would leave the room as if they had been fed a sort of energy drug. It was the fun and reward of learning new skills. I once heard John Kotter say "Learning gives a glow. Glow is good for folks". This is what Steve achieves in his work.

I very much like the way that the book is laid out in readily digestible 'chunks'. Over the years I have much enjoyed reading customer service books, which focus on employee motivation techniques. Some become too academic and theoretical. Steve's book is brilliant for the practical nature of his recommendations. I have been fortunate enough to see that they work. So often customer service is a leadership issue. People at the top often need quick sound bites to then be able to support their teams. This book is wonderful in this respect as well. It nudges bosses to play to peoples strengths.

This book is relevant for any era. This is an era where there is not any room to relax with margins under more pressure than ever. With much employee turnover in the retail world, customer service needs frequent re visiting. I have witnessed Steve provide excellent train the trainer work. This book complements this very well indeed. It will give the customer facing team the confidence to approach customers and develop relationships with their customers leading to improved business. The book is also very relevant to those who are not on the shop floor. They also need to understand the support that they can give. After all, those who are not serving the customer better be serving those who are!

I heartily recommend Steve's book to everyone involved in retail, healthcare or any organisation that needs to engage effectively with its customers and with its employees. Everyone can learn a lot from it.

Richard Wolff
Former International Retail Director
Marks and Spencer PLC

This is a book that could significantly increase the impact you, your teams and your organisation has internally and externally. It is full of practical ideas to create and sustain energy that will make a difference. And customers and colleagues will see, hear and feel the difference.

I have worked with Steve for many years and know that this works – employee engagement up, customer service up, revenue and margin up (or cost to serve down) and most important, customer, patient or internal stakeholder satisfaction materially improved.

Steve has a terrific attitude to learning and development. His expertise in the retail industry is very evident and all industries and functions can learn from retail at its best. The ideas in this book are easy to apply, fast, fun, scalable and cost effective. And when properly applied, lasting.

This book is packed with simple, practical concepts and exercises that work and is a terrific resource for people who really want to make a difference and not just read about it.

David Brown
Executive Director, Executive Education,
London Business School

WHAT IS THIS BOOK ABOUT?

This book, *Fired Up and Ready to Go!* is split into three parts which together make a comprehensive read about effective self management, techniques to engage effectively with customers and colleagues and sustaining a team to be fired up and ready to go so they can continue to engage effectively with their customers.

Part One is centred on getting yourself fired up and ready to go. It focuses on self management, detailing the results of 30 years' worth of my own personal experience and research, working with groups and listening to others strategies as to how they do this. It's not easy for any of us to remain at the top of our game day in day out but I have been particularly interested in those people that were able to do so and have tried to understand what were their enablers. It has become a comprehensive list of thoughts and ideas that I firmly believe if applied regularly and consistently, can help us all remain at the top of our game.

Once we are fired up and ready to go, Part Two describes the skills and behaviours you need to equip yourself with, in order to engage effectively with your customers and colleagues alike. Here there are some practical engagement skills that have been tried and tested with over 85,000 people over the last 16 years.

Part Three is targeted at leaders, managers and owner operators. This part of the book is designed to equip readers with the confidence and skills to sustain the momentum and keep their team fired up and ready to go. Part Three is centred on the importance of them as role models and the need for them to role model the behaviours that they want to see their teams demonstrating. As importantly, it focuses on the need for coaching as a way to ensure that team members are continually helped and supported to make the changes in behaviour needed to engage with customers and other colleagues effectively. In addition, I explore the need in Part Three truly to understand the customer needs from the customer's perspective, assessing how close you are to delivering those needs and building your activity around closing the gap. Finally, I cover the importance of recruiting the right people, measuring performance, process improvement and redesign.

PREFACE

They say everyone has one book in them. As my 50th birthday began to approach, I decided it was a great time to begin to reflect on my two careers: first as a retail manager and second as the managing partner of the training company Energize Learning.

I'd like to start off by sharing with you the experience of my first day in retail.

It was September 24th 1984, Marks and Spencer Bury branch – I was given my uniform, some till training and then I was sent down to the shop floor. Everything was going well that first morning – I remember thinking to myself "This is great!" I was shown how to order. I thought, "what more could there be to this retail thing?" But at 12 o'clock, I remember looking up and seeing what appeared to be a herd of customers heading towards my counter. I remember feeling a sense of immense panic.

What am I going to say to them? I thought. *They haven't trained me on that!*

Don't panic – think! I thought. *I know! What do people say to me when I go shopping?*

Got it, I thought – *They say can I help you?*

Do I like it when they say that to me? – No way! I thought.

But have I got anything else to use that would be better? – No.

So will I use it? – Yes ...

And did it work? No.

I'm convinced that this has gone on for years and years. People are told that they have to engage with customers but are not shown or told how to do so. Instead, what they are forced to do is to rely on their previous experience as customers and many times that previous experience involved them being asked, "Can I help you?"

So what I am about to share with you is my personal journey and how it started with that first day in retail back in 1984 and has continued on a journey that has led to me establishing and running Energize Learning.

We work with many organisations that are truly committed to driving a customer centric culture.

We do this by:

- Getting under the skin of an organisation to get an in-depth understanding of the organisation's culture.
- Understanding the customer's needs by talking to the customers and staff who engage with customers day in day out.
- Assessing those needs against the current customer experience to understand the gap.
- Developing workshops to enable the gap to be filled through behavioural and process change.
- Supporting leaders within the organisation to sustain the changes in the medium to long term.

Our interventions have been instrumental in helping to improve sales and conversion, transform service levels, increase employee engagement and reduce complaint levels.

The early years

Let's begin with the early years.

For me this started at the famous and indeed fabled retailer Marks and Spencer (M&S). While I was working at M&S I learnt about how to compile and interpret checking lists (stock status reports), stock replenishment, proportionate layout to maximise sales, driving effective promotions and returns per foot.

On top of which we used to get great breakfasts, lunch and afternoon tea upstairs in the catering unit as it was called. You could even get your hair done if you had any, which in those days, I did.

We were often lectured at to give great customer service, but in fact I don't remember ever being shown how. Instead, the approach was quite scientific and process-led. The emphasis was on knowing what was selling, what was coming in from the supplier and would we have enough of what was coming to meet the forecasts.

Having progressed rapidly from trainee manager to assistant manager at Marble Arch in London, I felt it was time to try my hand at merchandising at Head Office. After 18 months of crunching numbers and sitting in endless meetings, I decided it was time to move on and left that great organisation that was Marks and Spencer to discover if there was life outside of it.

"Show me the money"

Well it didn't take long to realise that there was in fact life outside Marks and Spencer, and I joined Coles Menswear, a much smaller company, in the early 1990s.

The reason for calling this period "Show me the money" was because the owner at the time, a man called Ronnie Cole, came to visit me on my first Saturday morning, while I was running his store at Brent Cross. I remember he said to me, "Go on approach that customer Steve! Has that customer been approached?"

Not only did Ronnie say this once, he must have repeated that dreaded phrase a dozen times. I began to think this must be the way to sell but I never really felt comfortable with it. On most occasions customers would respond by saying either:

"I'm fine thanks" or "I'm just looking thanks" Sometimes they just turned round and walked out the store.

I also spent some time working with Ronnie's son Keith, who ran the buying side of the business. Sadly, Coles didn't weather the recession of the 1990s and is no longer in existence but I am really grateful to Ronnie and Keith for this experience as it introduced me to the real world of selling and the competitive nature of sales people.

Story-telling

The third phase of my customer service journey began when I joined The Body Shop as regional manager and later rose to be head of retail. This culture felt much more comfortable to me and when I first joined, what I noticed in the shops was that the staff just talked to the customers about the products and told them the stories behind them.

This was progress I thought. It was at this point that I began to really understand the importance of the relationship between front-line staff and customers. It was also at this point that I was introduced to the term "Lifetime value of the customer." The way The Body Shop saw things was that whether a customer made a purchase that day or not, there was a huge opportunity for the front-line team to build a life-time relationship and therefore life-time value every time they interacted with a customer.

Unfortunately, by the early 1990s, other brands were jumping on the back of the natural toiletries and cosmetics market and customer numbers were falling. In addition to this, White Musk, Ananya and Dewberry – famous Body Shop sub-brands – were looking quite tired and Body Shop was not producing enough innovative new products to keep the customers interested and coming back. Customer numbers were dropping and this in turn led to falling sales.

It was at this point that Anita Roddick, Founder of The Body Shop, asked me to head up the Re-energize project. This was set up to re-energize the stores, which were looking tired to say the least.

Initially the project just focused on giving the stores a face lift in terms of shop fit and visual merchandise upgrade, but I realised that this alone was not going to solve the haemorrhaging of customer numbers. We also needed to re-energize the teams in the stores, who were working face to face with the customers every day.

At that time we measured the conversion rate in our 264 stores across the UK. It was running at 38%. In my head I began to wrestle not with the 38% who were making a purchase but the 62% who were not. In other words not the four out of ten that were buying but the six out of ten customers coming through the doors that were leaving with no purchase. We didn't need more customers through the door I thought, we just needed to help our front-line teams successfully engage with one or two more customers in a non-pushy way.

I realised at this point that it was not only a training issue that was needed, but instead it was a whole shift in mindset. We began to run selling and service days and went to work with a few regional managers on our shop floors and watched how customers reacted when we said and did different things. I can remember well, working in our flagship store on Oxford Street going up to customers and asking the usual questions. “Can I help you?” “Are you all right there?” “Do you need any help?” Not surprisingly I got the standard responses each time “No! I’m fine thanks”.

This not only made me realise we needed something else to say but also made me realise that when our staff received that response on numerous occasions, it dented their confidence. I wanted to give them some simple tools to help them engage with our customers in a natural way and in a fashion that would help to build their confidence. I was adamant that I didn’t want to introduce another programme that consisted of six or seven stages of the sale. It had to be simple, understandable to our front-line teams and most importantly, it needed to feel natural for our customers.

Over the next eighteen months, we developed a set of behaviours to be used by our front-line teams that customers truly appreciated. The results were staggering. In some stores we were able to put £1000’s of incremental sales in the till and overall we shifted the company conversion rate from 38 to 42%.

Very soon after that I decided to try out the principles in clothing and I was invited to work alongside a leading Franchisee for Levi Strauss in Manchester. Again, the results were staggering – Conversion went from 9% to 14% in just two days. I then had Levi Strauss keen to know what I had done and if we could replicate the same effect across their UK and European business.

The birth of Energize

It was at this point in January 2000, that Energize was born.

For the first five years after our foundation we worked with retailers, adapting what we had developed to suit the individual retailers’ business needs. Levi Strauss, Dockers and Adams Childrenswear were our first clients. We were then asked by Luc Vandevelde the CEO at Marks and Spencer at the time, to develop a version of our programme that would help them re-connect with their customer. This was a great success and very soon afterwards, we were asked to cascade our programme to over 55,000 staff across their whole UK business, within an 18-month period. The momentum was building and later that year we developed another version for their International business. This version went on to win a customer service award within their franchise business in the Middle East.

This early win certainly helped open the door to subsequent retailers such as Selfridges, Debenhams and Tesco, and has continued over the last sixteen years. More recently we have supported Liberty, Hugo Boss, Crew Clothing, Smith's News, Toys R Us and Bare Escentuals. To date, we have now worked with over 100 well known retail brands and over 85,000 area managers, front-line store managers and their teams.

In 2004 I was invited to meet with Heather Lawrence who was at that time, the CEO of Chelsea and Westminster Hospital. Heather was passionate about creating a service culture that would mean all her customers, the patients would have a good experience. Although unsure we could help initially, after spending time with Heather and her board discussing what behaviours they were wanting to see between colleagues and patients and colleagues and other colleagues, we were then able to develop a bespoke programme to help them.

This programme was rolled out to all 2,500 consultants, doctors, nurses and colleagues and supported them along their journey to be granted Foundation Trust status. In addition another award was picked up for their innovative customer experience programme. This confirmed for me that the types of programmes we delivered were not just relevant to retail sector but had a place in other sectors. We continued to work in the Healthcare sector and rolled out programmes of a similar nature for Jane Collins, chief executive and her team at Great Ormond Street Hospital and Haringey Primary Care Trust (PCT) and for Julia Brown chief operating officer and her team at Enfield Primary Care Trust. Word then spread as it had in retail and we continued this work for other trusts and PCTs.

It has been a real privilege to have worked with so many outstanding doctors, nurses and support staff at Great Ormond Street hospital, Chelsea and Westminster Hospital, Enfield, Haringey and Croydon PCT. All the healthcare professionals with whom we worked understood the importance of what we were doing and they were committed to ensuring that their teams were operating at the top of their game so they could engage positively and effectively with their patients and each other.

At a similar time, as the workstream started within healthcare we were invited by Richard Scudamore, CEO of the Premier Football League, to help him improve the levels of service at each of their clubs. He was concerned that ticket prices were rising and numbers through the gates were falling. He was also adamant that fans needed to have a really great experience when they went to watch a match or they would just stay home and watch it on television. This was a real eye opener for us as the challenges at the clubs were very different depending on how well the teams were performing.

If the clubs were playing well and in the top half of the league then their fans had great difficulty in getting hold of tickets. The front-line ticket office teams would often get abuse due to the fact the fans couldn't get hold of tickets and therefore couldn't go to the matches. We developed a programme to help those clubs focus on dealing with fans when there was a scarcity of tickets.

If, on the other hand the clubs were performing badly and were in the lower half of the league then ticket scarcity was not so much of an issue. Instead, the front-line ticket teams in those clubs received abuse about how badly the team were playing. It became clear the reason for this was those lovely people in the ticket office teams were the only people at the club to whom the fans could get exposure to and have a conversation with.

Since then, although retail remained and continues to remain our heritage and the heartland in which we operate, we have realised that our methods are applicable to many other sectors including private, public and leisure.

It was an absolute pleasure to have won a tender to work with the innovative Curo Housing Group – an amalgamation of several housing associations in the south west of England, making them one of the largest outside London. Curo not only talked about the need to deliver a great customer service to their customers but were determined to drive a culture that supported them to achieve their objective of being renowned for great customer service.

When an organisation sets itself up to be renowned for great customer service as Vic de Chuna, Donna Baddeley, Louise Swain and

Dominic Lynch did at Curo, it becomes a pleasure to support them to realise that ambition. They were all great role models!

More recently we have supported Smiths News, and their joint venture with Amazon, to launch their new parcel delivery service. With customers being ever-increasingly demanding, this has given them the opportunity to order their goods online and pick them up from their local convenience store within the same day. The beauty of this service is that the convenience stores open long hours and therefore customers do not have to remain home all morning or even all day to have a parcel delivered.

For a more extensive list of whom we are proud to have worked with and supported over the last 15 years, please refer to Appendix 3.

PART ONE

GETTING YOURSELF "FIRED UP AND READY TO GO"

1

INTRODUCTION

While the methods we developed within The Body Shop continue to have a positive impact on our clients sales and service levels, I noticed quite early on in our journey that the parts of our programmes that focused on helping senior leaders, managers and colleagues to feel fired up and ready to go appeared to be of particular benefit to many people on a personal level. This became the case in every marketplace in which we worked.

At the same time, I also became particularly interested in the relationship between high productivity and high self-esteem. The first part of this book therefore is dedicated to the importance of why should we bother to be fired up and ready to go and how to get ourselves fired up and ready to go each morning when we get up, get ready and go to work.

The fundamental and vitally important truth of the matter is this: once we are upbeat, positive and motivated we are far more able to engage effectively with our customers and each other. Too many staff today are quite simply not fired up and it shows. So use the ideas below to help you get “fired up and ready to go” not only at work but also in your personal lives.

Why bother, what’s the point you may be thinking? Well think about it. We spend on average eight hours a day working, two to three hours a day getting ready for work and travelling to and from work, and we sleep for eight hours if we are lucky. Last time I looked there was not a lot of time left for anything else. So I have reached the conclusion that whatever we do during our waking day, we may as well enjoy it! Being fired up and ready to go not only gives us a better chance of enjoying the day but it effects everything from how we feel to how we interact with friends, colleagues, customers and loved ones.

2

MOTHERS AND THEIR SONS

So let's begin with a short story at the start of a day. I need you to imagine that you are a fly on the wall watching a mother as she attempts to get her son out of bed and get him ready to go to school.

"John get up it's time to go to school."

Silence!

About five minutes later, John's mum shouts: "John, John get up its time to go to school."

Again silence!

So John's mum goes into John's room, sits on the end of his bed and shakes him. She then says "Come on John, you are going to be late. It's time to get up and get ready to go to school."

John grunts at his mother, rolls over and attempts to go back to sleep.

So John's mum shakes him and repeats: "John get up you are going to be late."

John finally sits up and looks at his mum and says: "Mum, there are six hundred kids in that school and not one of them likes me. There are thirty five teachers in that school and not one of them likes me either. Give me one good reason why I should get up and go to school?"

John's mum looks at him as only a mother could in that situation and says: "John I will give you two good reasons. One, you are 45 years old and two, you are the head teacher!!!"

The reason why I tell this story is not to make fun of teachers, head teachers or the education system but, to illustrate the point that in a survey, two out of three people declared that they do not like to get up in the morning. They do not like to get up and go to work. The reason for this is very often, where they work is not always an empowering, validating, supporting and nurturing place to be.

Let's be honest now, if we think about it, life generally is not always an empowering, validating, and a supporting place to be at times. Instead it's hard and can often feel like we are on a treadmill not really achieving anything and in the worse case we feel like we are running uphill or moving backwards.

So how can we feel good about ourselves? How can we be the best that we can be in a place that does not always support what we are trying to do? How can we respond to our customers and colleagues in a positive way when they do not always respond to us in that way?

Well let's explore this whole subject matter by getting you to imagine the following:

3

I DON'T LIKE MONDAYS

"There is little difference in people, but that little difference makes a big difference. The little difference is attitude. The big difference is whether it is positive or negative"
Clement Stone

Imagine you are tucked up in bed. It's a Monday morning, freezing cold and the middle of winter. The alarm goes off and you think to yourself.

"I am still so tired. Here we go again, another Monday, I really do not want to get up. It's so warm here in bed."

Eventually you drag yourself out of bed, go over to the curtains, look out and you think "I knew it, it's raining. It's going to be a bad day today. I remember last Monday when it rained, it was a bad day then, so it's bound to be a bad day today as well."

You then go downstairs to get some breakfast, open the fridge and guess what? No milk! Or worse the milk is off!

Many of us then turn on the radio or television and we get our daily dosage of the news – corruption, murder, war, cut backs, another leadership election, redundancies, earthquakes, etc etc.. It's all bad!

You have not even left your house or flat yet and you have started sliding down your personal Spiral.

(N.B. Your personal Spiral is a reflection of how you are feeling over the course of a day)

Some of us then get in the car and the car won't start. When it does finally start, within minutes you are stuck in traffic and thinking that you are going to be late for work. Or you get on the train, tube or bus and there are no seats and you are packed in like sardines. You end up standing next to someone who has had garlic the night before and they really stink.

You finally get to work and say to a colleague "Hi, How are you today?" What do they say?

"You don't want to know the sort of morning I have had!" You then think to yourself, wow they have got out of bed the wrong side today. Quietly you move on and get yourself organised for work. Meanwhile, you can hear others saying the same sort of thing.

In retail we go on the shop floor and are immediately faced with stock or staff problems. Everybody then moans about stock or staff for ten minutes and then go further down their Spiral.

In offices we are constantly faced with IT issues or new initiatives from HR – so everybody talks about that and go further down the Spiral.

Everywhere we go we always have people not turning up due to sickness. This then means that your workload has just doubled for the day.

Before you know it, it's the end of the day and the whole team have crashed at the bottom of the Spiral.

The picture I just painted, was one where the whole team reached the bottom of the Spiral at the end of the day. We go into a lot of different organisations, many times the colleagues within those organisations find themselves at the bottom of their Spiral at 9'clock in the morning.

When we stand back and really think about it, the thing that brings people down the Spiral is how we respond to what happens to us during the day. It is our response to the events that take place during the day that bring us down the Spiral, that in turn affects how we feel during the day and affects our ability to engage with both customers and our other colleagues.

But it doesn't have to be like this. Let me explain why.

Imagine you have a day off. It's mid week and you have the house or flat to yourself. You think you will do a few odd jobs during the morning. In the afternoon you decide that you will put your feet up and watch your favourite film.

It's mid afternoon, you are watching the film, when suddenly you hear a noise outside, one that comes from a truck when it's reversing.

You look outside and there is a rubbish truck with all the rubbish from the local neighbourhood reversing up your drive towards your front door.

The next thing the driver dumps all his rubbish just by your front door step. What would you then do? This is a multiple-choice question.

1. Ignore it and go back to watching your film, or
2. Get out there and sort him out?

I suspect the answer to that would be 2.

Let's now go back to work. Isn't it strange that we wouldn't allow anybody to pour rubbish on our doorstep, but we allow people to pour rubbish another word for negativity into our brains every day of our lives. The trouble with this is that if all we are hearing is negativity around us, there is a high possibility that we will become infected and we will be negative ourselves.

We have discovered that teams who work hard together to stay at the top of the Spiral, have a better day, a more enjoyable day, one that goes quicker and what's more the customer notices it because there is a better atmosphere in that environment.

We believe that nobody can, has or will ever be able to choose your attitude for you. Only you can choose your attitude. It is always your choice.

So think about the Spiral, think about where you want to be on it. Remember however, that wherever you are on it is down to your choice.

People are always saying to me they get the Spiral and that we choose our own attitude but it's tough out there. How can we stay up the top of the Spiral or how can we choose the right attitude every day?

We have run many sessions over the last sixteen years, where we share best ways to stay upbeat, positive and motivated to enable us to stay at the top of the Spiral and to enable us to make the right choices when responding to what happens to us during the day. I have outlined a list of our favourites in the following chapters.

4

DECIDE WHAT TO FOCUS ON

What you focus on is what you get. I'll say that again – what you focus on is what you get. So if you focus on the negative that's what you will get. If on the other hand you focus on the positive that's what you get also.

If I said to you now "Do not think of elephants!" how many of you, even if it was just for a second saw an elephant? Or if I said the dog is not chasing the cat, how many of you saw a dog chasing the cat? The mind does not hear the negative and just hears the command – think of elephants or the dog is chasing the cat.

If I said to you let's have a bad day, I bet if I fast-forwarded the day to the end of the day I would hear someone saying "told you, bad day." But if I said let's have a great day. What are the chances of having a better day? Yes that's right, a better chance.

How many times have you decided you need a new big ticket item, it may be a car or a holiday, then every time the radio is on there is an advert for that very item? Or if it's a car then every time you walk down the street you see the very model in the very colour that you want. Why does that happen? It happens because you are focusing on and therefore receptive to these particular things. These things are always around us, but when we decide we need them or decide to focus on them, we notice them more often..

People say to me this is great and we feel really motivated but how do you keep that feeling going. My answer is always the same and that is to monitor your thoughts and monitor your language – that's the thoughts and language you use with yourself and the thoughts and language you use with other people. Let me give you an example.

Imagine this scene:

It's a Monday morning. It's about 6.30a.m.You're still asleep, nice and warm in your bed.

The alarm goes off! You get yourself up out of bed. You walk across to the curtains and you open them and look outside. It's a beautiful day, the sun is shining, the sky is blue and you think it's going to be a great day.

You walk across to the wardrobe to get your shirt/blouse. It's all ironed so you get yourself ready. You then go downstairs to get some breakfast. You open the fridge and remember you've bought a fabulous breakfast which you then prepare and begin to eat. Whilst you're eating your breakfast you might listen to the radio and you hear your favourite song, which then sticks in your head for the next few hours.

You then get your coat on and make your way to work. You get outside and feel the sun down on your back and it's a great feeling. The birds are singing and you think again about how good you feel. The journey to work goes like clockwork and you get all the right connections with no delays. You arrive at work!

A colleague meets you at the door and says "Hi, how are you today?" and you reply, "Great."

If we were to keep up the positive language internally and externally i.e. what we say to ourselves and to other people, we would have a better chance of feeling positive for longer.

What we think about and what we talk about affects how we feel. Who decides what we think about and what we talk about? We do!

So you can decide how you ultimately feel and if you want to feel positive, upbeat and motivated then think about being upbeat, positive and motivated. You see many of us have got into the habit of thinking negative thoughts and talking using negative words so if we want to change this, we need to break the habit.

I urge you to start today. Be part of a new generation. Start by getting up and saying to yourself: "I'm going to have a great day. I'm going to make a difference" instead of "Oh no, here we go again!"

Be aware of those people around you and their language. Notice if it's negative. If it is, move away from that particular person. Spend time with positive people. Try this for a week and write a log at the end of each day of what you observed.

5

CHOOSE YOUR RESPONSE

"No one can make me feel inferior without my consent,"
Eleanor Roosevelt

Many of us go through life blaming others and blaming circumstances for how we behave and how we feel. This is quite common and it allows us not to have to take responsibility for what happens to us.

I was a witness to an exercise run with a group of fifteen senior managers in Sofia, Bulgaria, a few years ago. The facilitator asked the group to all stand in the corner of the room and throw a crunched-up piece of paper into a waste paper basket that he had placed at the other end of the room. The only rule was that they all had to throw it at the same time.

There was a brief moment of excitement as the facilitator counted down from five to one and at that point everyone attempted to throw their piece of paper into the basket. The result was not great. In fact only one piece of paper out of fifteen landed on target. Everyone was then asked to sit down and the facilitator quickly prepared a flip chart with two columns, the one on the left was headed external and the one on the right internal.

He then asked the group, with the exception of the person who succeeded, to explain why they had not been successful in throwing their piece of paper into the waste paper basket. As the group declared their reasons he charted them up as follows:

External	Internal
• The paper was too light. • The bin was too far away. • The other people put me off. • The air conditioning knocked me off course. • The bin was too small. • The facilitator did not give me time to practise. • The paper was too thin. • The light was shining in my eyes.	• I did not aim correctly.

He then asked them if they realised what was happening and after a few minutes the group admitted that they were blaming other things and other people for their failure. In other words, they were blaming external factors for the result that they had got. Only one comment listed under the internal column represented the individual taking personal responsibility.

The truth of the matter however is this: although we are not always responsible for what happens to us, we are definitely responsible for how we respond to what happens to us and how we respond determines how we feel.

Let me share with you an example to prove the point above. Let's say I came up to you (bearing in mind I have never met you before) and say that you are the biggest idiot I have ever met in my life. You then have several choices how you respond. You could respond by thinking how did he figure it out so quickly? Then how are you going to feel? Pretty bad I would suspect. You may even go inside yourself and find evidence to support how you feel. However, you could also respond in a different way, saying to yourself that you have never met me before and you know for a fact that you are in no way an idiot. If you responded in that way you will probably at worst feel neutral. You certainly wouldn't feel bad. We are therefore in control of how we respond and therefore how we feel.

If we look at the theory behind what we are discussing above it may look something like this:

E + R = O

E = the events in your life
R = your response to those events
O = the outcome that you experience

To summarise, the events in your life plus your response to those events will determine the outcome that you experience.

Unlike animals, humans have a slight gap after the E (event) and before the R (response). This slight gap gives us the ability to choose our response and being able to choose our response enables us to determine the outcome that we experience.

Let us now consider some real life events and the different responses that are available to us all.

Flight delay example

First response

- Event – Flight is delayed.
- Response – Get angry for missing valuable time of holiday.
- Outcome – Feel disappointment, frustration and anger.

Second response

- Event – Flight is delayed.
- Response – Decide to enjoy time with partner and catch up with them.
- Outcome – Feel relaxed and calm.

Job application example

First response

- Event – Unsuccessful job interview.
- Response – You start to doubt your ability.
- Outcome – Your confidence takes a hit.

Second response

- Event – Unsuccessful job interview.
- Response – Request feedback so you can learn where you went wrong.
- Outcome – Understand where you went wrong and increase chance of future success.

Now the above examples have happened to many of us in our lifetime. However people respond differently to the same event and as a result experience a very different outcome.

At a deeper level it is interesting how when we grieve after the loss of a relative or close friend, some people move on emotionally more rapidly than others. This has to be down to when the individual chooses a different response and chooses to move on with their life.

Now if we agree with this theory, and it takes responsibility to do so, we can never blame people again for making us feel anything. It's not what people do or say but it's how we respond to what they do or say that determines how we feel.

"No one can make me feel inferior without my consent." (Eleanor Roosevelt)

This quote by Eleanor Roosevelt reconfirms this point perfectly. It's how I respond that determines how I feel.

I once met a lady called Joanne a few years ago when delivering one of our programmes for one of our clients.

Joanne sat in one of my workshops. She didn't contribute and you could tell from her whole demeanour that she was quite negative. She sat at the back of the room, with her arms crossed not talking to anybody. In fact I found out later on that she was known as the store 'mood hoover', as she would suck the life out of everybody and drag the whole team down. I could however tell once the workshop started, that she was listening as she was nodding and making eye contact with me. It was an afternoon session and finished close to the end of the day. Joanne went home as did I.

The next morning I was scheduled to be back in that store coaching on the shop floor. When I arrived, the manager came running up to me asking me if I had seen Joanne. For a moment I was worried and thought that maybe she had left the business. The manager soon alleviated my fears and explained she hadn't left the business and that I should go and see her on the shop floor.

So I went to find Joanne and I found her chatting in a very friendly way, with a big smile on her face, to the rest of the staff. I asked her what happened to her and she simply explained how she had found my session very interesting especially the part about the Spiral.

She said she had gone home after the session in the usual way and there he was (her husband) sat watching the TV waiting for his dinner. He then spent the whole time, while they were eating, being negative about his day and his job. Then he started to be negative about Joanne's day and her job.

Nervously, I then asked what happened next. I say 'nervously' because it was one of those moments when because of how she was talking you think momentarily that she may have finished him off. Thankfully she hadn't and instead she explained that she had said the following to him.

"Listen here you Neg. You are not bringing me down my Spiral ever again."

Well you can imagine her husband looking at her not having a clue what she was talking about as he had not attended the training session.

She went on to explain that for weeks it had been the same pattern. She had got home and there he was being negative about his day and his job, then he turned on Joanne and was negative about her day and her job. This in turn she explained, was causing her to be negative. She then went to bed feeling negative, woke up feeling negative and then she would just bring that negativity into work every day and spread it around.

The Spiral, she explained, had taught her that she has a choice how she responds. The Spiral taught her that when she gets up in the morning she can choose whether or not to have a bad day or a good day. She realised for the first time in many months that she could choose how she responded to her husband's bad mood. That day, rather than being stuck feeling negative, she decided to have a good day.

For me what was really powerful was not only had it awakened an awareness in Joanne that the choice was hers, but also the impact that it had had on the team. It's really easy for one person to bring down the mood within the team. That day Joanne was having the opposite effect in that she was helping to create a positive atmosphere within the team.

Now Joanne uses different language, doesn't drop grenades into conversations and chooses to stay at the top of her personal Spiral. For those interested, she is still married.

6

THE POWER OF THOUGHTS

Put your hand up if you talk to yourself? Whenever I ask groups that question, 80-90% of the audience put their hands up straight away. I can usually see the rest thinking to themselves "Do I talk to myself? I don't know do I talk to myself?"

Psychologists tell us we think over 55,000 thoughts a day and many of those thoughts are about ourselves, how we are doing, how we are feeling? what we think of other people, what they think of us etc. etc.. If our thoughts are constantly positive there is a pretty good chance of us feeling good. However, if those thoughts are constantly negative there is equally a good chance of us feeling anxious or down or low. Therefore we can conclude if we want to feel good about ourselves, (and by the way when we do feel good we are more likely to have better interactions with other people) we need to be thinking more positive thoughts than negative thoughts.

Now many of our thought patterns were developed and set at a very early age. So if any of you have/had parents or grandparents that would say things like "What would you want to do that for?" or more specifically, "What do you want to go and live in London for? You will never come back?" (Mine were right by the way) Another common one, "the grass isn't always greener you know", it is understandable why we think the way we think. But like all bad habits, with a bit of work, they can be broken.

I always advise people to become more aware of what they are thinking about when they first wake up in the morning and when they are about to go to bed at night. If your thoughts are negative at the start of the day, it is likely that the rest of the day will follow suit. It's almost as if you are setting the rudder for the day and that's the direction you will end up going. If on the other hand you think of something that makes you laugh or smile or makes you feel good, that too is setting the rudder for your day and there is a much greater likelihood that you will go on to have a good day.

What happens by making a conscious decision to think positively is that you will then break the cycle. It is a fact you cannot think of a positive at the same time of thinking of a negative. (Men can't anyway as I'm reliably informed we cannot multi-task) So if you catch yourself thinking negatively my advice to you is try and flick the switch and make a conscious decision just to think positively.

7

DO WE SPEAK THE SAME LANGUAGE?

The language we use can also have a huge impact on ourselves and others around us. Many times I have noticed that when I am in the company of a negative person I walk away feeling drained. Negative people like to drop grenades into conversations. Basic comments like "Here we go again!" or "That won't work" can leave a team or individuals flattened. It's really important therefore that we are aware of our own language and the language of others around us.

I find it really interesting when I meet a new group for the first time. I listen very carefully to the language taking place prior to the beginning of the workshop or seminar. Invariably it's negative and about the difficulty of their journey or the bad weather. I have often wondered if it might be because people like to be part of the "Isn't it awful" club.

The time I spent working in schools was fascinating. I would have expected the language in the staffroom to be positive, but in actual fact it was the opposite. Now I don't want to categorise all teachers' staffrooms as the same but it must be very worrying for those of us with children if our teachers are in that negative mindset, as this will certainly have an impact on our children.

I'm still waiting to hear "I feel great and delighted to be alive" – How different would that make us feel? Perhaps that's just a bit optimistic for the reserved conservative culture in which we live.

Barack Obama tells a great story. Back in September 2009 during his election campaign when he was presenting to a large group of students at the University of Maryland. His message behind this story was about the power of positive language.

The story was about a visit he had made to the state of Greenwood South Carolina for a district meeting. He had promised that he would go to visit there and in return he would get the vote from the state representative.

What he didn't realise was that it was approximately one and a half hours from most other places so it wasn't as if he could just go there on the way to somewhere else. So he tells the story of how he got up very early in the morning, looked out of his window and it was pouring with rain, opened the newspaper and there was a bad article written about him. He hadn't even left his hotel room and he talked about how bad he felt, and how he wasn't looking forward to this trip to Greenwood.

Eventually he got to the district building in Greenwood South Carolina and there were only twenty people there to see him and they didn't seem to be too pleased to be there either on that cold wet morning.

He began shaking hands with everyone and then suddenly he heard a voice behind him call out "Fired Up", and everyone just replied back "Fired up" as if it was the norm. He looked round and saw a short lady in her 50's wearing a church hat looking directly at him and smiling while she then shouted "Ready to go", and everyone in the room replied "Ready to Go" again as if it was just the norm.

Unaware of what was happening, this carried on for the next five minutes with this lady shouting "Fired up" and the crowd of twenty replying "Fired up" then shouting "Ready to go" and the crowd replying "Ready to go". He looked around at his staff to see if they knew what was going on but it appeared that they did not know what was going on either.

He went on to say what was really interesting was that after a few minutes he started to join in and within another few minutes he started to feel fired up and ready to go – much better than feeling wet, cold, tired and damp which was how he had been feeling the whole journey down to Greenwood.

Barack Obama went on to say that if a voice could change a room, then it could certainly change a state, and if it could change a state, then it could certainly change a country, and if it could change a country, then it could certainly change a nation.

He went on to say "We need your voice to change this nation. We need the voice of young people to change this nation. So tell me are you fired up?" The crowd who were on their feet at this point screamed back "Fired Up". "Are you ready to go?" he shouted and the crowd screamed back "Ready to go". Fired up, Fired up, Ready to go, Ready to go.

For me the lesson we can take from this is that it reinforces how much of an impact positive language can have not only in a room of just twenty people but as demonstrated by Barack Obama on another occasion, in a stadium of 5,000 young people.

I liked the story so much, and felt the point it made really captured the impact positive language can have, that I decided to name this book after it.

8

FOCUS ON YOUR STRENGTHS, SUCCESSES AND ACHIEVEMENTS

The main thing that holds children and indeed adults back is our lack of self-belief. Focusing on strengths, successes and achievements really helps us to feel positive about ourselves and increases our willingness to reach out, take some risks and learn some new things.

During the early years of Energize, I was also an LEA Governor for a local secondary school. I was invited to create and carry out some workshops around building self-confidence. After some careful thought I created workshops that were aimed at helping school children visualise and re-affirm their strengths and successes.

We invited the children to create self-portraits of themselves and then their friends and families wrote on their self-portraits everything they loved about them, everything they were good at and basically as many positive things about them as they could think of. It was so powerful to see and hear the positive things that friends and family had said about these children.

When the workshop finished, the classroom teacher who was working alongside me at the time decided to stick all the self -portraits on the classroom wall. This reminded them each day of all the good stuff they had heard about themselves. What a great idea that was to surround them with all these great re-enforcing comments. These portraits stayed stuck up on the wall until the end of the year.

What was even more powerful was the lasting impact that it had on the children. They constantly talked about and referred back to the workshop. I'm convinced it was for many of them the first time that they had spent time hearing about the great things that those close to them actually thought about them.

When we worked with George Davis who was launching Per Una in Marks and Spencer in 2003, he was keen for the colleagues on the front-line to feel confident about themselves when selling his new ranges.

It appeared to me that we could adapt the work we had carried out in schools and run it for those Marks and Spencer colleagues selling Per Una. It worked brilliantly. The colleagues loved it and it really helped them to feel successful and confident in themselves.

Since then we have carried out this self-portrait workshop for many clients with great success. In recent years we have developed this further by getting colleagues to think about it for their teams. It really does help to unite a team and get them feeling proud to be part of it.

Getting teams to create a team strength list, success board and talk about why it is good to be part of the team helps create a positive environment and it becomes a great visual reminder of what a great place to work they have.

A few years ago, many years after we first began running workshops on this subject matter, I bumped into a delegate who had attended one of our workshops. We were both pleased to meet each other again. Once we had established who we both were and where we had met before, she pulled a piece of paper out of her purse. At first I was a bit confused as to what it was but she soon explained it to me. It turned out that she had been so taken with the self-portrait exercise, immediately after the event she had transferred all the positive comments her colleagues had written about her onto a small piece of paper so that it would fit neatly into her purse. She went on to explain how she took it out from time to time and it gave her a real boost and reminded her of how great she felt that afternoon when she took part in the workshop.

Individual Exercise – success log

Set up a success log. Every time you have a success, however small, jot it down in the success log. Whenever you are about to do something for the first time that feels scary pick up the success log and remind yourself about how good you really are.

Exercise – Focus on your achievements

Spend time thinking about what you have achieved. Many of us write a list for the week or the day and cross off the items we have achieved. What's left at the end of the day is just transferred over to the next day. We never really get to appreciate what we have achieved. Try ticking the items you have achieved and crossing out the ones that need transferring over. This way you get to only see the items you have achieved.

Group Exercise – Self-Portraits

Ask the group to each draw a large picture of their faces on a piece of flip chart paper. This picture should be as colourful as possible and the group should be given at least 15 minutes to do this. Once all the group have drawn their pictures ask them all in turn to write one or two positive things on each colleague's picture.

Focus on Successes

As well as focusing on your strengths you should remind yourself of your successes, however small you might feel them to be.

I once attended a conference where they aimed to do exactly that – get people to focus on their successes. They started off by asking us all to split our lives into thirds – easy for me at that time as I had just turned 30. Once we had done that they asked us to consider each third really carefully and note down all the successes we had in that first third. Now to begin with this appeared really difficult as there were lots of things that we just take for granted. For example – learnt to walk, learnt to talk, learnt to count, learnt to write etc....

We were then asked to repeat the same process for the second third and the final third. Although it took some time and some deep soul searching, eventually it started flowing and it was amazing to recall all the successes we had had in our life time.

We went round the group talking about our successes and listening to the others in the group and it was really uplifting.

The next stage of the conference was to think about the next section of our lives that we were entering into and start to write down all the successes that we wanted to have during this period. Again everyone went to work thinking about future ambitions, writing them down, then declaring them to the group. This time we had to talk through why it was so important to us to succeed in these things. The more reasons we could think of for having these future successes the more compelling they became.

Now I always keep that list to hand. When I am about to do something that will take me out of my comfort zone, I allow myself a quick glance at the successes I have had in my life so far. It really does help to put me into a resourceful state and help me feel a little bit better to go and do what I am about to do.

One other nugget I gleaned from this conference was that they talked to us about displaying our successes so that we could see them every day. They believed that in doing so you were constantly reminding yourself of the fact that you were successful.

Now to be honest, when I was growing up I used to go round to friends' houses and see golf or football trophies in cabinets in the hallways. I used to think it was quite strange and thought that their parents who were displaying their trophies in what seemed to me a boastful way were terribly egotistical.. Now I understand that what they were doing consciously or subconsciously was that they were reminding themselves of how successful they were every time they walked past these displays.

If you now visit my office, I have the few trophies that I have won over the years on my window sill next to my desk and pictures of my family, friends and loved ones. It certainly works for me and helps me remain in a positive resourceful state.

Exercise – Successes

I would strongly suggest that you repeat this exercise yourself. It does not have to be done in a large group; it can simply be done on your own. To remind you of how it works follow the simple steps below:

1. *Simply split your life into thirds.*

2. *Take the first third and list down all the successes you have had within this period. Don't take anything for granted. The more you can think of the more empowering it becomes.*
3. *Next take the second third. This always appears to be the hardest one to remember for some reason. Keep at it and eventually you will find that they will start flowing.*
4. *Next on to the final third. Again keep at it until they start flowing.*
5. *Finally think about the next part of your life and ask yourself what successes would you like to have in this next period of your life. Once you have a comprehensive list, next to each of the successes, note down why these would be important. Remember the more reasons you can find the more compelling they become and the greater the likelihood that you will achieve them.*

9

VISUALISE A DESIRABLE OUTCOME

Here we use a technique known as Future Pacing. Visualising the future in a way that we would like it is a powerful technique. When we hear people say "I cannot see myself doing that, you could put a safe bet on the fact that they probably won't do it. On the other hand helping people visualise the future they want creates a much clearer route of what they have to do in order to get there.

Exercise – Future Pacing

With the help of music, close your eyes and relax. Breathe slowly in through the nose and out through the mouth. Become aware of your breathing and allow your thoughts to drift away. As those thoughts come back in, just push them away. Now imagine you are going to a place in the future where you have achieved what you hope to achieve. It may be passing exams, making friends, being selected for your football team or getting the job you have always wanted.

Once you have a clear picture notice what it looks like, listen to what it sounds like and become aware of how it feels. Allow yourself time to do this. Notice what you can see, what you can hear, the voices or noises around you and become aware of how good it feels.

Now notice what you can see as it becomes five times brighter, be aware of what you can hear as the sounds around you become five times louder and feel what you can feel as it becomes five times more compelling. Then imagine that you are at the top of a mountain that you have successfully climbed, look over the top and notice the route you followed to get there. This is a very different experience to standing at the bottom of the mountain and looking up to the top to work out the route you need to follow to get to the top.

Now I would like you to repeat the whole process. Imagine you are going to a place in the future where you have achieved what you hope to achieve. It may be passing exams, making friends, being selected for your football team or getting the job you have always wanted. Once you have a clear idea of what it looks like, listen to what it sounds like and become aware of how it feels. Allow yourself time to do this. Notice what you can see, notice what you can hear, the voices or noises around you and become aware of how good it feels.

Now notice what you can see as it becomes ten times brighter, be aware of what you can hear as the sounds around you become ten times louder and feel what you can feel as the whole thing becomes ten times more compelling.

Then as if you are at the top of a mountain that you have successfully climbed, look over the top and notice the route you followed to get there.

Whilst you have this desired future absolutely clear in your mind a technique known as anchoring can be used at this point to ensure that you recall everything you saw, heard and felt once you had achieved what you wanted to achieve. Creating an anchor is simple. When you can really see, feel and hear how it is when you have achieved what you want to achieve touch a part of your arm firmly for a few seconds.

When you want to recall what it looks, sounds and feels like again in the future, just close your eyes and relax again. Breathe slowly in through the nose and out through the mouth. Become aware of your breathing and allow your thoughts to drift away. As those thoughts come back in just push them away. Now touch the same place on your arm and the picture, sounds and feelings of the desired future you had created should come back instantly.

10

DIET, HYDRATION AND EXERCISE

In 2004 I was invited to attend an Anthony Robbins seminar at a huge venue at the 02 Arena in London. Whilst I was sceptical at first of these mass motivational seminars, I was touched by two things in particular.

One was the fire walk where Anthony Robbins managed to persuade 5000 people to march bare foot across burning hot coals. Thinking that he had in some way hypnotised us all I had another go just to make sure. It was a really powerful metaphor for confronting fears as not many people believe they could walk across burning coals without harming themselves.

The other was the final day that was dedicated to diet, hydration and exercise. This for me had the most profound impact.

Consciously thinking of what and how I was eating and drinking enabled me to lose almost twenty pounds. I began a gentle running programme and this further helped to get me in better shape. In addition I started to replace the copious amounts of coffee I would drink in a day with water.

I then started to notice that I began to feel I had more energy and also I felt stronger. It was interesting also that my best ideas came to me when I was running. I made a conscious decision this January just gone to reduce my alcohol intake to zero for the month. I thought doing so would make me feel better. This it did, but the most surprising thing for me was how much better I slept during the month.

We all know much has been written on the subject areas of diet and exercise. Exercise in particular releases endorphins in the brain and these in turn help us to feel better. It is important therefore that you find some form of exercise that suits you. It does not have to be time consuming or expensive, it can be just regular walking or

30 minutes worth of exercise at home. It just needs to be regular in order to feel the benefits.

I have come to the conclusion that being conscious of what you eat and drink and taking gentle regular exercise helps to keep you healthy. The greatest challenge is having that conscious awareness and then sustaining the habit.

11

RELAXATION

Relaxation is a great way to feel refreshed and stay at the top of your game and ensure that you are fired up and ready to go. As with many things today there are many different types of techniques to help us relax.

Many of us use exercise as a form of relaxation and a way to release the tensions of the day. Yoga is a great way to exercise and clear the mind at the same time. For those of us that do not have access to Yoga studios or exercise classes there are simple techniques that we can use at home that can help us relax too.

Exercise – Simple relaxation exercise

Below is a useful exercise for relaxing. It is especially helpful if you need to calm down and clear your mind.

1. *Sit down comfortably, somewhere where you won't be disturbed.*
2. *Close your eyes and focus on breathing slowly in through your nose and out through your mouth.*
3. *Now allow your mind to wander. Lots of thoughts will very likely pop into your mind. Try to avoid paying attention to them and instead concentrate on your breathing – in through your nose and out through your mouth.*
4. *As more thoughts come into your mind, just push them away and concentrate again on your breathing. In through your nose and out through your mouth.*
5. *After about five minutes or so, think about starting to open your eyes while continuing to concentrate on your breathing.*
6. *Notice how relaxed and refreshed you now feel and when you are ready, stand up and slowly begin your activities.*

12

MUSIC

I attended a seminar recently where they asked me what my favourite song was. At first I was confused with the question until they explained it was the song that made me feel inspired or motivated. On reflection, I realised I had a few that I liked for different reasons. We then went on to discuss one by one what our song was and why.

The client I was working with at that time was going through a transformation programme, and asked the question of all the delegates.

They then started to play extracts from different songs during the breaks at this seminar. It was fascinating to see how the music instantly lifted the energy in the room. People began moving and dancing to the songs that they liked and recognised.

Now whenever I enter a workshop or seminar where there is no music, I notice that there is a different atmosphere and a different energy in the room.

Music can also be used to bring a more positive state of mind, helping to keep depression and anxiety at bay. This can help prevent the stress response from wreaking havoc on the body, and can help keep creativity and optimism levels higher, bringing many other benefits.

Research has shown that music has a profound effect on your body and psyche. In fact, there's a growing field of health care known as music therapy, which uses music to heal. Those who practice music therapy are finding a benefit in using music to help children with attention deficit hyperactivity disorder (ADHD), and hospitals are beginning to use music and music therapy to help with pain management, to help ward off depression, to promote movement, to calm patients, to ease muscle tension, and for many other advantages that music and music therapy can bring.

This is not surprising, as music affects the body and mind in many powerful ways.

So my advice to you is make sure you have music in your life not only at home but at work too if it does not exist already. Get your teams to talk about their anthems and then create a list and play them whenever it is appropriate to do so. Notice the energy it produces.

13

BUILD THE DESIRE

"Determine that the thing shall be done, and then we shall find the way."
Abraham Lincoln

I would like to welcome you all to my new home sales team. We sell expensive products at discounted prices. I'd like you to imagine please that you have left your current job, have applied and interviewed successfully to become part of this new sales team.

Our first task today is to sell these beautiful crystal vases. Now normally they retail for £500 but we have done a deal with a company in a far away country and have bought a container load. In fact we have bought so many that we can afford to go out and sell them for the greatly reduced price of £200 each. We are therefore talking about a huge discount.

Now how many of you think you could sell four hundred of these over the next four weeks (that's one hundred per week) and for each one you sell we will give you £1.

When I ask my groups this question the response I get is pretty much always the same. There is a general lack of reaction and people just look at me in a disappointed and suspicious manner.

However, when I then ask the same group, how many of you think you could sell four hundred of these over the next four weeks (that's one hundred per week) and if you can you will get £5000? The answer is always 100% yes from everybody.

When I ask what the difference between the two was? the responses vary from motivation, money, £5000, etc.

That may well be the case but if we really think about it the main reason why the second request gets 100% yes is down to our Desire!!!

In the first example you were probably working out whom you were going to sell them to but as soon as you heard the magic figure of £1 you thought to yourself no way. I'm not getting out of bed for that. What is the point?

But when you heard the magic figure of £5000, you did not even think about whom you were going to sell them to, or how you were going to sell them, you just knew you were going to sell them.

You don't need to know how you're going to do it. If the desire is strong enough, you will find a way. You see if the desire is strong enough, you can do anything in life.

And right now you might not be 100% sure as to how you are going to be the best you can be and achieve all your goals and live the life that you dream of but let me assure you that:

If the desire is strong enough you will find a way.

14

RELEASE THE PAST

"If you think you can or you think you cannot you are right."
Henry Ford

"If you always do what you have always done, you will always get what you have always got."
Henry Ford

The Baby Elephant Story

How many of you have ever been to the circus or seen the circus on television? If you have you may remember an act with elephants. Often elephants would be led round and round the circus ring one behind the other. When the trainer wanted the elephants to stop they would tie a thin cord around the lead elephants back leg, tie the other end of the cord to a thin cane and then simply stick the cane in a bucket of sand. The lead elephant would then stand perfectly still and the rest of the elephants would follow suit. I used to wonder why the lead elephant wouldn't just keep going. After all an adult elephant weighs up to four tons and could just take off.

The reason why it doesn't just run off is because of the way many elephants used to be trained. When it was a baby elephant, as soon as it could stand up and walk, a huge rope would be tied around its back leg while the other end of the rope was tied to a tree trunk. For days the baby elephant would pull and pull and pull and as it could not get away it would eventually just give up.

Then anytime later in life when anything is placed around its back leg, it just goes back to its previous experience (i.e. not being able to get away) and so it doesn't even bother trying.

The elephant lets previous experience affect it later in life. It allows what happened to it in the past to prevent it from even trying to get away. If we are honest we can all be a bit like that.

The reason why I tell you this story is to demonstrate to you and urge you not to let anything that has happened to you or that you have done in the past (and which hasn't worked out how you would have wished) stop you from trying it again or trying other things in the future.

Sometimes you just need to believe fervently in yourself. The elephant could clearly have run a mile with its strength as an adult. The reason it didn't was not because it was not able but because of past conditioning. Its past conditioning was that it simply believed it wasn't able to escape from something from which it could, in fact, have escaped easily.

In order to move forward in life it is essential to let go of things that have happened to us in the past that now prevent us from moving forward.

Group Exercise

I discovered the following exercise whilst I was working in schools. I think it is a really helpful tool for letting go of beliefs that we have, that are not very useful to us. Beliefs that we hold that are stopping us move forward. It can be done on your own or as part of a group exercise.

Ask everyone in the group to list down all the things that they believe they can't do, are not very good at or don't believe they can do well. Let this exercise go on for at least 15 minutes.

Ask everyone then to fold their list up and bring them to the front where they have to place them in a small cardboard box.

Ask the group to then follow you outside where you proceed to bury the box.

And recite the following eulogy for "I can't".

Friends, we are gathered here today to honour the memory of "I can't".

While I can't was with us on this earth, he touched the lives of everyone, some more than others. Unfortunately his name has been mentioned in many places.

We have provided "I can't" with a final resting place. He is survived by his brothers and sisters "I can" "I will" and "I'm going to do it right away". They are not as well known as their relative and certainly are not as strong or as powerful yet. Perhaps with your help they will make an even bigger mark on the world.

May "I can't" rest in peace and may everyone present pick up their lives and move forward. Amen.

This eulogy is a metaphor for letting go of unhelpful beliefs and helps us picture this exercise whenever we hear the word I can't.

So think carefully about all the things you are not happy with in your life and challenge yourself as to what you have done/ continue to do that may be the reason why you are attracting these things towards you.

On a more practical level it is worth considering doing some if not all of the following:

Clear out your house, flat, car, shed, office, wardrobe or desk. Have you ever noticed how good it feels when you spend some time clearing out one of the above?

I firmly believe that you feel so good about doing this because when you clear something out you allow room for something new.

Shortly after our first child was born I remember my wife, Kathryn, complaining that she had nothing to wear. When I looked at her big double wardrobe I noticed it was jam packed full mainly with maternity clothes that she had been wearing for the last nine months. Once she had taken all the clothes out that no longer fitted her, she was able to make room for some new clothes, which she subsequently went on to buy.

Acknowledge and let go of relationships/friendships that are over. During our life journey we meet lots of different people and form lots of relationships with them. The reality is that some of these relationships are short term and are due to the current circumstances that we may be in at that time, and some are long term and stay with us for many years.

There are also those that have run their course but we feel bad about letting them finish. It could be because our kids are still friendly with their kids or our partners get on well. The reality is that whilst they remain within our inner sphere there is little room for new friendships to develop.

In addition, if these friendships leave you feeling drained then it is important that you let go of them in a human sensitive way.

Forgive people who have hurt you in the past

Many of us hold grudges for many years for things that the people have done or said to us. It may feel a little petty to go and forgive them in person. The chances are they may not even have remembered what they had said or done. Another way of forgiving them is to write a letter to them without actually sending it. Just by putting ink to paper can be sufficient to let go of it.

15

TAKE ACTION

"You cannot discover new oceans unless you have the courage to lose sight of the shore."
Andre Gide

"Feel the fear and do it anyway."
Susan Jeffers

One of the most important steps in all this insight is taking action. There is no point with any amount of planning and positive thinking, if no action is taken. There is never a shortage of thoughts and ideas. What there is often a shortage of is action.

So think about what you want, agree what you are going to do and then begin to do it. We are often put off starting something new, difficult or scary for fear that we may not be successful. If we don't start we cannot be unsuccessful. We very rarely get it right first time but taking action is the first step in getting going and feedback helps us to see if we are on track or not.

When I first set up Energize in 2000, I was extremely committed to setting up my own company to support others to drive sales, average spend and conversion within the retail sector.

I can remember lots of people asking me what my strategy was and answering I didn't really have one. I also remember seeing the look in their eyes that said – "He hasn't got a chance." But what I did do was take action. I got out there, knocked on doors, sold my ideas to as many people as would listen to me, listened to their feedback and the business began to come in.

I believe that was because I didn't have all the answers, I didn't have it all worked out, but I did take action and every time I went off track, I listened to the feedback and got back on track.

During the time we were working in schools helping to build confidence and self-esteem, I often talked about the importance of coming up with great ideas as well as the importance of action.

Right at the end of the workshop, to check everyone had understood the point of taking action I would parade around the room holding up a £10 note. I would ask who would like this £10 note and immediately many hands would shoot up with great enthusiasm. After all, most children regard £10 as quite a lot of money. I would then ask why each person should have it and there then followed a stream of creative ideas of why each individual person should qualify to have the £10 note.

We would go round the group and each person would attempt to persuade me that they deserved the £10 note. I need it for some sweets, I would share it with everyone, I would give it to charity – We had many wonderful creative, heartfelt ideas. Round and round we would go, sometimes the exercise would go round the whole group several times.

Sometimes I had to get really close to each child, almost putting the £10 under their nose. It was usually at this point that one person would just take it from my hand. When the disappointment from everyone else had subsided, I would then ask what got the £10 note and you would feel the frustration in the room when everyone realised that what got it was that the person took action. Everyone had good ideas I would explain but only one person was brave enough to take action and actually take it from my hand.

In many groups children would shout out that they had thought about doing that but explained that they had felt embarrassed or that it would be rude to just take it. I would explain again that there is never a shortage of ideas, but there is a shortage of people taking a leap of faith which sometimes means stepping outside our comfort zone, feeling rude or embarrassed and taking action.

I think taking action is one of the key lessons many people take from our workshops and seminars.

Taking action in many cases can be scary. In many cases it prevents people from taking the smallest first step.

In her book *Feel The Fear And Do It Anyway,* Susan Jeffers skillfully shows how to break the cycle of inaction and argues the only way to work through the fear is by feeling the fear and doing it anyway.

As a young manager I was once invited to make a presentation to a senior manager. I had at the time had experience of presenting to groups at my local youth group and set out to prepare. What I failed to prepare for was the questions that might be asked.

As I began to deliver my presentation I was asked a few questions that totally knocked me off track. This became like a chain around my leg. Every time I was asked or had the opportunity again to make a presentation, I did everything possible to avoid it. This went on for years until I read Susan Jeffers book.

Once I realised everyone has the same feelings and that those feelings never go away entirely they just become less extreme, I was able to move forward.

An interesting article in the medical journal The Lancet, displayed the results of a survey. They asked a large group of people what they feared most in life.

I was surprised to see that public speaking was on the list as number one, while death was number three. It seemed to me bizarre that people would rather die than get up in front of a group and speak. Yet I know that many people do think like that.

So if you need to but find it difficult to stand up in front of groups of people, I strongly suggest you aim to feel the fear and do it anyway. For those of you who need to take action but are being held back for some sort of fear, feel the fear and do it anyway. You will be so energised when you do. This energy will help to carry you through and fuel the energy and motivation to keep going and do more things that are scary and uncomfortable.

16

PERSEVERE AND LISTEN FOR FEEDBACK

"Never, never, never, give up."
Sir Winston Churchill

The biggest single reason for failure to achieve what we want to achieve, is because we give up when it gets hard. Or we give up as soon as we encounter the first hurdle or obstacle. Hurdles and obstacles should be seen as feedback or as the universe telling us we haven't got it quite right or that we are moving in the wrong direction. We should see this as a positive piece of feedback as it helps us get back on track.

It is imperative that we understand the art of perseverance. Think about it. If it was easy everybody would be doing it. Things that are really meaningful, that will quantum leap us into a new phase or take us to a new level are nine times out of ten hard to achieve.

Imagine I ask you to strike a nail into a piece of wood using this hammer. I only allow you one strike. Unless you are very talented indeed at DIY, what are the chances of you getting the nail right into the centre of the piece of wood so the head of the nail is sitting flush with the piece of wood? No chance I hear you say.

Instead, it would obviously be much easier to get the result you require by making many small, well-judged taps that end up driving the nail into the wood with careful precision.

So my advice to you with all of what I have been sharing with you so far is to go and practice tapping away until you get the result you want. Try it out and give yourself time to master the ideas. Do not get disillusioned if it doesn't work for you the first time, instead try it again and again until you notice some changes. Just like the story above about the piece of wood many things involving a change in behaviour take time to practise and time to master.

So persevere – why? because it will be worth it in the end.

Listen for feedback

We only know if we are on track by listening out for feedback.

The real challenge though is to ensure that we take feedback in a positive way and learn from it. Traditionally if someone says I need to give you some feedback our first reaction is why? what is the matter? or what have I done wrong?

If you have ever had the chance to sail a boat, you are taught to focus on a point in the distance where you wish to travel. You then set off with your eye fixed on the point in the distance that you have set as your destination. Within a few seconds you will notice that you are off track and therefore you will alter the sail to change direction to get back on track. Within a few more minutes the same thing will have happened, i.e. you will be off track again. So you alter the sail again and get back on track again. The reality however is that you will be off track much more than you will be on track. What is important is that you respond to being off track and attempt to steer the sailing boat back on track. If you don't you will find that you will end up miles off course. If you do not set sail until the wind is exactly the speed and direction you need for it to take you straight to your destination, the chances are you would never leave the shore.

So it is really important to embrace feedback as a positive way to ensure that we get back on course and to ensure that we are heading in the right direction to get where we want to get to.

When a co-pilot or navigator tells the pilot in a plane to change direction by a certain degree, the captain doesn't say to himself why? What have I done wrong? Instead what he does say to the navigator or co-pilot, is thank you, and then takes the necessary action. Just like with the sailing boat if he didn't take the appropriate action, he too would end up way off course.

17

CELEBRATE SUCCESS AND THANK THOSE THAT HELPED

"Let us be grateful to people who make us happy; they are the charming gardeners who make our souls blossom."
Marcel Proust

When you have achieved what you wanted to achieve do not forget about the effort that went into it. Instead it's really important to recognise how far you have come and celebrate your success. Even if there are mini-successes along the way. There is no point in waiting until we have arrived at exactly where we want to end up as we will be waiting a long time. Celebrating along the way gives us added momentum and ideas for continuing.

Thank those that helped you along the way

So once you are fired up and ready to go and achieving what you want to achieve, make a list of all the people that helped you along the way. This is also known as the attitude of gratitude.

It is very often forgotten once we get on our journey, but it is really important. Spend time really thinking about who has helped you. People really appreciate being thanked. When they are, they are then more inclined to help you again in the future.

One's journey through life is never straightforward. We all need help and advice from others. People who feel appreciated will want to help you so make sure you show them appreciation.

It doesn't really matter how you thank someone, it's the thought that counts. The fact that you took the time to tell someone you are grateful for what they did or are doing is the point. Don't deliberate too long on deciding which medium is best. As long as your message is genuine, it will be appreciated.

You might be surprised to learn that most people don't receive thank you messages all that often. It'll make them feel fantastic when they receive your kind words, guaranteed.

A thank-you note is not only a great way to be remembered, but also to be introduced. Whether it's a speaker at an event that you didn't get the chance to meet in person, or the author of a book that inspired you, thanking people is a great way to get on their radar and make that personal connection.

Being grateful for what you have received and expressing that to others will bring other positive things into your life. You will be more aware of how others impact you, and will want to return the favour. That positive and appreciative attitude will make you attract more good things.

With an attitude of gratitude you will make the people around you feel appreciated, and with that will come a wealth of personal connections and opportunities.

PART TWO

FIRED UP AND READY TO GO TO PUT YOUR CUSTOMER FIRST

18

INTRODUCTION

So if we acknowledge that it is down to us to ensure that we are fired up and ready to go, let's now start to examine HOW we can make a difference with our customers and ensure that we put them first. How should we behave with them so that they have a great experience and wish to come back time and time again.

A good starting-point is to consider how we like to be treated when we visit a public or private organisation.

Group Exercise

Let's start off with an exercise called "Love and the Loathe".

Split the group into two – one group becomes the "Love" group, the other group becomes the "Loathe" group

The "Love" group should chart up how they like to be treated by a member of staff when they visit a restaurant, retail shop or public place.

The "Loathe" group should chart up how they do not like (loathe) to be treated by a member of staff when they visit a restaurant, retail shop or public place.

It is important to emphasise that it is how you are treated and not any of the physical aspects of the particular environment.

Both groups then present their work back to the rest of the group. Our experience shows us that the "Love" groups usually come up with items similar to our "Love" list below:

- *Being greeted.*
- *Acknowledged.*
- *Smile.*
- *Eye contact.*
- *Friendly staff.*

- *Helpful staff.*
- *Honest staff.*

The "Loathe" groups usually come up with items similar to our "Loathe" list below:

- *Being ignored.*
- *Jumped on.*
- *Pushy staff.*
- *Staff talking among themselves.*
- *Staff chewing gum.*
- *Staff texting on their phone.*
- *Staff being rude.*

Key points

When we ask groups which they would prefer when they engage with different organisations, the answer is always what is on the "Love" list.

When we ask them is there anything stopping them giving their customers what's on their "Love" list the answer is always no.

When we ask them do they think anyone in any of the organisations where they experience what is on the "Loathe" group is telling their employees to give their customers what is on the "Loathe" list, the answer is always no.

So why do we ever experience what is on the "Loathe" list when nobody is telling staff to behave this way and everyone can do what is on the "Love" list?

I believe it must come down to choice. No one is telling staff to behave in the "Loathe" way and nothing is stopping them behave in the "Love" way. It must therefore come down to choice.

Can you imagine if every front-line member of staff chose to give what is on the love list, would your customer receive a good customer experience? Would there be a good atmosphere in that particular place? Would sales or service levels go up or down?

Hundreds and thousands of pounds are spent by organisations in every sector every year on training staff to behave in the right way with their customers. Hours and hours of time are given over to this whole subject matter. So why at best do we get a mixture of both what is on the "Love" list and the "Loathe" list?

I believe that at heart this isn't about training. People cannot be trained in how to smile, or how to be helpful or friendly. Instead they have to make a choice themselves. They have to make a conscious decision each day when they come to work whether they are helpful and friendly or miserable and grumpy. So how can we get everybody to choose to do what is on the love list every time, when let's be honest, working in most work environments can be tough. Every workplace has its pressures.

Imagine if we invited all the chief executives and managing directors of the top hundred or so businesses in the country to come to discuss their offer of customer service. If we asked them what sort of service do their organisations offer, what do you think they would say?

My guess would be that they would respond by saying that their organisations give great service. It is their number one priority and they invest thousands of pounds into training their staff. The reality however is what we experience day in day out. At best we get a mixture of what is written on the love and loathe lists. Every night their business will bank money and in many cases a substantial amount of money.

Think about it for a minute. How much more could they be banking if they treated their customers better? Currently, in many cases they are taking money without even trying. Are they really creating lifetime customers who will want to come back again and again?

The next chapters outline for those serious about giving great service to their customers, how to engage effectively with customers of any organisation so that they make purchases, tell others and come back again and again.

19

LIVING OUR CUSTOMER FIRST

How many times have you entered a retail environment, public building or restaurant and either been ignored or served in an aggressive and pushy way? Either way it does not lead to an enjoyable or memorable experience. Very often staff are so involved in their tasks, you could explode and they would not notice you.

Let's prioritise the following four essential topics on the shop floor in retail.

1. Visual merchandising.
2. Team.
3. Customer.
4. Tasks.

When we ask groups to put in order of priority the four things above, most say customer should be the number one priority. In fact, in 99% of cases, the response we get is that customer and team are number one and number two. There is often a debate about tasks and merchandising and we tend to reach agreement around these two as joint third. But let's go back to the first two.

Now as I said, the customer usually comes out first, but sometimes we get quite passionate individuals that will argue that it's the team. They go on to argue that without them (the team) there is no one to serve the customer and ultimately we will have no business. That may well be true but if you have the best team in the world, the best at service, the best at stock, the best at merchandising but no customers coming through your doors, what is going to happen the business? Yes we all agree that eventually it will close down.

So eventually, we reach the conclusion that the customer has to be our number one priority. However can we put our hands on our hearts and say that we live the customer first every time?

Now don't get me wrong, the tasks have to be done. The shop floor has to look inviting with great displays to grab your attention. But the bottom line is the customer has to come first. In many ways we need to get the balance right and this balance can be one of the hardest challenges that we all face in retail today.

Next time you are on the shop floor ask yourself this question. Where is my attention? Where ever your attention is at that moment in time, that is what you are living, as your number one priority.

We need to focus on the customer. We need to get the balance right. We need to live the customer first.

20

THE INITIAL GREETING

For years I would hear from my line managers that we must greet our customers but I would never hear how to do so. For years I would repeat the same thing to my teams. On reflection what I never heard about and what I never talked to my teams about was how to greet customers. The how was almost unimportant, but the how is the key. The how is what makes all the difference. My area management team and I cancelled all the usual countless meetings at Head Office and instead went back to the front-line on the shop floor at The Body Shop to find a way to address the falling customer numbers and help drive sales conversion.

Whilst intellectually we understood the need for greeting customers to ensure they felt relaxed and welcomed into our shops, we never equipped our staff with the how to greet them.

I can remember approaching and greeting customers as they entered our store on Oxford Street and asking them "Can I help you?" "Are you all right there?" "Do you need any help?" Interestingly I got the same response each time – "I'm fine thanks!" Sometimes they even turned towards the door and walked out. I'm convinced they did this because by saying "Can I help you?" to a customer, really means "Can I sell you something?"

Two things then became clear:

1. Customers do not respond well to that approach.
2. Each time a colleague gets that response from the customer, it knocks their confidence and makes them less inclined to attempt to engage with more customers.

I strongly believe this has gone on and continues to go on around the country in most retail organisations for years. We had to find a way that enabled us to greet our customers in a non- pushy way, that didn't elicit that all too common response – "I'm fine thanks."

So we set about trying to find a different way to engage with our customers. I always describe it to people as how we experimented with our customers. We said many different things to customers and watched their response to what we said.

Very early on we became aware that by just saying "hello" or "hi"in a sincere way, and ideally accompanied by a smile, had a positive effect.

It appeared to do the following:

- It broke down the barriers.
- It showed the customer they had been noticed.
- It made the customer feel at home.

In addition to this, we started to notice that if we just said "hello or hi", made eye contact and smiled at the customer we got a response from the customer. It was this response from the customer that was key. It was key because it told us so much about the customer at that moment in time.

We discovered that the customer would respond in one of two ways.

First response

We greeted the customer, made good eye contact and smiled.

The customer said "hello or hi" back and looked away.

We began to realise that if the customer said "hello or hi" back and looked away, it could mean various things:

- They knew what they wanted.
- They didn't want any help.
- They were shy.
- They were a shop lifter.
- Or it just meant that they were OK at that point.

It didn't mean that they had had a tough upbringing or were seeing a psychiatrist.

If we left the customer to browse at that point the chances of them coming back to us when they did need help were quite high. This was actually borne out many times. At the very least we had welcomed them into our store.

I have to add in most cases customers responded in this way. Let's face it when we go shopping we like to be greeted or welcomed but then most of us like to be given some space to browse and have a look around.

Second response

We greeted the customer, made good eye contact and smiled.

The customer said "hello or hi" back but then didn't look away.

This response was more interesting. We noticed that on average two out of ten customers said hello back but kept the eye contact with us. If at this point we were bold enough to say nothing, the customer then went on to ask us a question. In those situations the conversation then flowed naturally as we were not "selling" to the customer. Instead we were just responding to their needs.

We were suddenly engaged in conversation, a much more effective way to then go on and help the customer. In fact, we were not having to sell at all, as the customer asked us for what they were looking for. What I find amazing is that it is such a simple discovery but it has helped so many people because it means one does not have to bother with all the sophisticated types of sales and questioning techniques to engage in conversation with a potential customer in the first place.

What was even more remarkable was when I was invited by Heather Lawrence the CEO at the time of Chelsea and Westminster Hospital to work with her to improve the patient experience in her hospital, this technique worked as well as it had within a retail environment.

Very often her patients came into the hospital or were wandering around the hospital anxious, unsure or needing help. This technique, a simple hello, making of eye contact and a smile was all it took to alleviate peoples fears or anxiety and very often lead to them asking us a simple question, which was usually around location of certain departments.

Finally we spent many years supporting medical technology companies exhibiting at European Congresses helping their employees engage with neurosurgeons and other eminent doctors as they walked past the medical technology companies extremely expensive conference stands at congress. This same greeting technique helped them engage with many new customers which in turn led to a massive increase in the number of new inquiries for their life saving products.

Marta Gehring, Marketing Director for Medtronic Pain Therapies, said:

"You can really see the difference as a result of the Energize engagement training: Leads collected were up 600% on the previous event. The power of the training lay in its simplistic approach!"

One final point – Be careful to ensure the initial "hello or hi" is loud enough and once they are fully inside the hospital, store or office. There is, what we call a decompression zone or chamber that exists at the threshold of any business premises. If one attempts to engage while a customer is still walking through this zone, they may not acknowledge you. Alternatively if music is playing too loudly and we speak too quietly they may not hear our initial greeting.

21

THE DREADED APPROACH

As mentioned in the introduction my memory of the approach or "dreaded approach" as I call it dates back to my time at Coles Menswear when Ronnie Cole would wander around the store asking us all if this customer had been approached and if that customer had been approached. It felt so uncomfortable that we would take it in turns approaching the customers, get the usual knock back, then carry on with the tasks we had been set for the day, in our specific areas.

Trying to talk to a customer when they don't need help only leads to rejection of the colleague, frustration for the customer and most importantly the loss of the sale on that day and potentially forever.

In truth I could argue that you don't need to approach anyone. After all when you need help in a retail environment, restaurant or public place, what do you normally do? Most people say they look round for someone to help them and then go and ask them for help. If there is no one around to ask or the staff do not seem interested in helping then you consider walking out and going elsewhere. So, if we watch out for those that need help then get within their line of sight the chances are they will then see us and then ask us for help.

So what I'm eluding to is that what we should focus on is once we have greeted or welcomed our customers, we should then set about observing them and acting on those who begin to give signals that they might need help – In other words "approach signals."

Exercise – Approach signals

Make a list of all the signals that your customers display within your organisation that will indicate that they need help.

Let's now have a look at the signals you have come up with that tell us that your customer may need help:

Approach signals

- *Looking around.*
- *Looking confused.*
- *Looking for a member of staff to help.*
- *Looking through a rack for sizes.*
- *Holding stock up against themselves in the mirror.*
- *Saying to a friend, "I wonder if this comes in a medium".*
- *Saying to a friend, "I wonder if this comes in blue?"*
- *One person says to the other person ,"Just ask will you. Just ask that assistant!"*

So if those are the common approach signals, how should we then approach the customer?

Before making any approach we should just watch subtly from a distance, looking for the signals above that tell you the customer might need help. If we just approach everyone – the spray gun approach, the chance of engaging with them at the right time is quite slim.

When you see any of the signals listed above, move within the customers line of sight. The customer will often do as we all do when we need help and that is just ask. When this happens, you are then easily engaged with the customer because they have approached and asked for help from you.

Alternatively other successful methods include the idea of working your way to the side of the customer leaving at least five feet between you and the customer. If you just tidy the stock or clean a counter whilst you are doing this, you and the customer will both feel comfortable. In many cases the customer will then ask you a question.

Now there are cases when we might misread the signals or the customer is shy. If they don't ask you a question, there is no harm in making a positive comment about the item they seem to be interested in or a positive comment about something in general. Asking if you can help them at this point may come across as pushy and tends to push the customers away.

Summary of the approach

When you see a customer giving off an approach signal; move over to the left or to the right of the customer.

Avoid walking straight up to the customer. Fold or tidy some clothes as if you are doing a task.

When you get to about five feet away from the customer, stop, but keep tidying. The customer will become aware of you from the corner of their eye. From this point the customer will just be aware of you tidying the stock.

Wait a few seconds to see if the customer asks you a question. If they don't simply say 'hello", make eye contact and smile.

If the customer says 'hello' back and then looks away, they are ok. If they continue to hold eye contact, they will ask you a question.

22

ASKING GREAT QUESTIONS

So once we have identified approach signals, what do we say to our customers if they don't ask us a question? Asking questions will help you build rapport with your customers and in turn this will help to understand their needs.

If we are not careful, we may ask the wrong type of question or alternatively, we may blind the customer with too many questions.

Below I have selected a few key types of questions that if asked, will help you easily identify the needs of your customers:

Open questions

These types of questions open up the conversation and are really useful when starting a conversation with a customer. They help to reveal the customer's opinions, feelings and thoughts.

Examples of open questions are:

- How can I help you?
- Perhaps you could tell me something about the person you are buying for?
- Which designs do you like best?
- What look are you trying to achieve?
- What do you need it to do?
- Tell me about the occasion you are buying for?

Probing questions

These types of questions allow us to get more specific information from the customer. With more technical products, probing questions help to narrow down the choices you may then go on to offer your customer. Asking probing questions helps to elicit information that may not have been obtained from your initial open questions.

Examples of probing questions are:

- Which specific brands does he/she like?
- Which specific colour do you prefer?
- Why do you think that?
- Why do you believe that to be the case?
- What other features are important to you?
- What other functions would be helpful to you?

Understanding questions

'Understanding' types of questions allow us to check we have fully understood what the customer has said and at the same time asking such questions demonstrates to our customers that we have listened to their needs.

Examples of understanding questions are:

- So you need a party outfit and one that can double up for work. Is that right?
- What I understand is that you need it to have the capacity to print 50 sheets of paper per minute. Is that correct?
- So what you are saying is you washed the item using the instructions given and it has discoloured. Is that right?

Closed questions

These types of questions help you take control of the conversation. In many cases they help to bring the conversation to an end or help you to facilitate the customer to make a decision.

Examples of closed questions are:

- Would you prefer this model or that model?
- Would you like us to fix your current product or find you a replacement?
- Shall we go and talk with him now?
- Would you like this capacity or that capacity?
- Would you prefer a refund or a replacement?

If you were to "google" question types you will find that there are many types of questions. What I think is important it that you have a toolkit containing a few questions of each type. This way you will firstly be able to remember them and secondly be able to draw on them when you need them.

Questioning Skills – consolidation exercise

What types of questions are each of the following?

1. *Shall we go and talk with him now?*
2. *How do you feel it is going?*
3. *So what you are saying is.........Is that right?*
4. *Why do you think that?*
5. *Would you like this option or that?*
6. *Please tell me about what happened?*
7. *What would you like to happen next?*

Answers

1. *Closed.*
2. *Open.*
3. *Checking understanding.*
4. *Probing.*
5. *Closed.*
6. *Open.*
7. *Probing.*

23

LISTENING SKILLS

"Seek first to understand, then be understood"
Stephen Covey

In his book *The Seven Habits of Highly Effective People* Stephen Covey dedicates an entire chapter to the subject of listening. He explains how, of all the habits that he discovered were common in highly effective people, their ability to listen was a vitally important one.

Listening is the key to understanding and can be the key to a great customer experience and in the long term it will determine whether you create lifetime customers for your business.

Listening skills should never be underestimated. The better we are at listening the more able we will be to build rapport and long-term relationships with our customers.

Listening Exercise

Turn and face a partner and ask them to share a story with you. The story can be about anything that you are able to talk freely about for a minute or so. For the first thirty seconds your job is to show no interest at all. Ask your partner at the end of the thirty seconds to tell you what that felt like for them i.e. not being listened to.

These are some of the feelings we have when we feel we are not being listened to:

- *Embarrassed.*
- *Felt like stopping.*
- *Felt like I was boring.*
- *Frustrated.*

- *Stupid.*
- *Insulted.*

Now face the partner again and ask them to repeat the story. This time listen to them like your life depends on it. Ask them to notice what you did different the second time that signalled to them that you were really listening.

When people are truly listening they:

- *Make eye contact.*
- *Smile.*
- *Nod.*
- *Lean forward.*
- *Ask questions.*
- *Comment on what has been said.*

Now repeat the process, changing roles so the other person gets to experience what it feels like when they are not listened to and to notice what someone does that demonstrates they are listening well.

As I mentioned earlier, we think more than 55,000 thoughts a day. I often describe that as the 'background conversation'. We often think we are listening but our own background conversations can often be turned up so high, that in fact, we miss vital information.

When we don't listen, the consequences are that we leave people with many negative feelings including embarrassment, frustration and inadequacy. If our customers feel any of these we greatly reduce the likelihood of a sale today or any time in the future. In order to listen effectively therefore we need to turn down our background conversation. Now this can be difficult and it takes effort especially if our background conversation is on full volume.

In addition we need to make good eye contact, nod to demonstrate we are really listening, ask questions and make comments. Most importantly we must ensure that the customer is doing most of the talking.

Another thing to be aware of when we are listening to our

customers is to concentrate hard on not making assumptions that will hinder our interaction with them. Most of us have seen that famous scene in the film Pretty Woman when Julia Roberts is treated disrespectfully by the shop assistant as someone who has no money and is not worth spending the time with. How wrong was that assistant when Julia Roberts walked back in with Richard Gere and proceeded to buy almost everything in the shop but from the other assistant, who would enjoy the enormous commission!

We make assumptions based on how people speak, look and based on our previous experiences. While we all do this naturally, if we are not careful and aware, it can work to our disadvantage. We should therefore work hard to make sure we resist making assumptions about our customers.

Group Exercise

Ask the group who thinks they are good at listening. We usually get one or two volunteers put their hands up. Ask the rest of the group to leave the room. The volunteer is then given the following information verbally:

Mr Smith from Chalk Industries is arriving into Paddington at 10.30am from Dorchester. If he has not arrived at the office by 11am, please send a car to pick him up.

The volunteer then is requested to pass this information onto one of the other members of the group who are instructed to come in one by one. Each person then has to pass on what they heard without writing anything down, without asking any questions and with only hearing the instruction once.

The last person then declares to the group what they have heard and this is compared to the original instruction. I have not had a group yet where the last person's version in anyway compares to the original instruction.

The group is then asked what would have helped them remember the instruction more accurately?

The following points are then noted:

- *Write down key/important points including names, times and places.*
- *Ask questions to clarify understanding.*
- *Ask them to repeat it.*

In a call centre environment, the three points above are critical for ensuring that telephone operators accurately understand their callers.

24

BENEFITS AND FEATURES VERSES FEELINGS

We know that the more benefits and features the customer is aware of the greater the likelihood that they will buy. Imagine a set of scales in front of you. If the benefits and features are on one side and the barriers to the sale are on the other, we simply have to ensure that the scales are weighted in favour of the benefits and features in order to make the sale.

In addition to this it has been discovered that if a customer has positive feeling towards a service or product then this far outweighs the features and benefits and makes it much easier to push the scales over to the purchase side of the balance.

Introducing language that will help the customer feel positive towards the product or service therefore will greatly help in tipping the scale towards making the decision to purchase.

Examples of language that will help a customer feel positive towards a particular product or service are as follows:

- Imagine how relaxed you will feel when using it.
- Just think how good you will feel, seeing the delight on her face when she first opens it.
- Imagine the wonderful lasting memory it will create for both of you.
- Picture how happy you will feel as people compliment you on your great taste.

Those of you that remember the famous John Lewis Christmas adverts will remember them not for their specific products but for the feeling they left you with. Many adverts play on the emotions that you will experience when owning or using such and such a product not the product itself.

Remember also that people buy the result or benefit that the particular product or service will give them. So customers buy clothes to look good or look a particular way. People buy drinks to quench their thirst or a lawn mower to have a neat lawn not necessarily because they enjoy mowing the lawn, but instead the result that it provides them with.

So introduce language that will help the customer feel positive or good about the result of the item or service they are interested in and the scales will move in your favour.

25

LINK SELLING

Link selling or as it is often known "add-on sales" is when the sales person introduces another item that complements or enhances the product the customer is about to buy.

It has a reputation for being pushy and one that customers do not like. It doesn't have to be like that, though. Imagine that you have gone out to buy a new television. You have done some research online but wish to go and look at it in the flesh before you make your final purchase.

When you get to the store you find a very helpful colleague who informs you that the model you are hoping to purchase is on special offer in this store and there is stock available to take it home today. You decide to purchase it, pay for the television, thank the colleague for his help and set off for home. When you get home and begin to set up the television you realise that it has not come with a bracket to fix it to the wall. You then have to go out again and take another trip to your local store to purchase a bracket, which is frustrating and time consuming.

If the colleague in the original store you visited had checked where you intended to display the television and had pointed out that it did not contain a wall bracket, would you have been happy to purchase one? Probably yes. So it's important that we see link selling as a method that helps to enhance the product or service the customer is about to buy.

We forget that retailers sell thousands of products which we in those businesses know all about and which are all displayed around the store. Many customers however only see a small selection as they go round a particular store or from store to store. They very often become blind to the rails and rails of merchandise that are on display. So we have to tell them about the other products, particularly the ones that could enhance or complement the one they are about to buy.

To avoid the situation described above and if we want our customers to know about the other lines that we sell, we simply have to tell them. Link selling allows us to introduce other products that we sell that our customers may not know about but may well need.

I would like to share with you two guidelines for introducing link selling:

The first guideline concerns timing. If we try and introduce another product, that complements the product the customer has come in for, before they have decided on the first product, there is a high chance that it will come over to the customer as pushy and not only will they reject the additional product but they might also reject the original product.

So if we had introduced the wall bracket before the customer had made his mind up about the television, the customer may have felt we were being pushy and then left the store without making a purchase. It is really important that we wait until the customer tells us that they are going to purchase the product that they originally came in for, or that they indicate strongly to us that this is the case.

The second rule is about association. The product we introduce must complement the product the customer is about to buy. Once the customer indicates they are happy to buy the product we have helped them with, we can introduce a product that complements or enhances the product or service the customer is about to buy. Again, in this case, as the customer was intending to mount the television on the wall, introducing the bracket at this point would have been extremely useful to the customer and would have saved him or her much time and frustration. It is highly unlikely that the customer would have rejected the original product, the television saying:

"I'm not having that television now because you tried to sell me a wall bracket."

The worst that could have happened if you had checked if they needed a wall bracket when they indicated they wished to purchase the television, was that they might have said "No thanks, I have a wall bracket at home."

What we are also doing is planting the seed in the customers mind and letting them know about many of the products that we sell that they may not know about. What we find time and time again is that when we have helped a customer and have built good rapport with them, they are much more willing to listen to our suggestions and ideas for other items that they might need.

Link Selling Exercise

Part One

A useful exercise is to get teams to think about the most popular items that they currently sell together. This helps less experienced team members and gives them the ideas for what they can introduce together.

Examples of common link sales are:

- *Coffee and a croissant.*
- *Necklace and earrings.*
- *Television and wall bracket.*
- *Camera and memory card.*
- *Laptop and case.*
- *Sandwich and a drink.*

The list is essentially endless but it is really helpful to have a good knowledge of the most popular ones in your business.

Part Two

Once you have a list of the most popular link sales, the team can then brainstorm the most effective comments or questions they could ask the customer to introduce the most popular link sales.
Examples:

- *Our croissants are delicious and fresh, would you like one with your coffee this morning?*

- *The cream cakes are fabulous, would you like one with your tea?*
- *These earrings go beautifully with the necklace you have chosen.*
- *You said you were planning to wall mount the television, can I show you the brackets we have available?*
- *What size memory card would you like?*
- *Shall I show you our sturdy cases that will help to protect your new laptop?*
- *Would you like a refreshing drink with your sandwich?*

26

DEALING WITH OBJECTIONS TO THE SALE

It always surprises me to watch the response from groups when we discuss dealing with objections to the sale. We always begin with working through the different type of objections across the range of products or services. Inevitably we always get people talking about complaints. For the purpose of clarity this section is dedicated to how to respond when a customer puts up objections to buying the item or items that we have presented to them.

To begin with, however, we should take a moment to try and understand why our customers may not see things in the same way as we do. Well, the simple answer is that we are all different, we have been brought up differently and we have experienced the world in different ways. Based on all these different experiences we see the world through different lenses. How we perceive the world therefore is our own reality.

Sales people who have their own lenses believe how they see the world and its parts is the right way. We need to be careful because if we try and persuade a customer that what they see is wrong we are in danger of:

- Breaking the rapport we have built with them.
- Causing them to feel frustrated with us.
- Risking not converting the sale.

Effective salespeople use three simple steps when a customer presents an objection to making a purchase.

1. Acknowledge or thank the customer for bringing it to your attention.

2. Discuss the rationale for a particular issue including benefits, features and feelings.
3. Ask a question around the benefits, features or feelings you have pointed out.

Example One

The customer objects to the price of a pair of leather shoes.

Acknowledge or thank
Many customers raise the same point that they feel they are a little expensive.

Rationale
Our shoes are made from highest quality leather and then treated to ensure that the leather softens with age. This means that you get a really comfortable long lasting fit.

Question
How important is it to you that your shoes remain comfortable over a long period of time?

Example Two

The customer objects to the price of the cashmere sweater.

Acknowledge or thank
That's a good point you raise and one that is quite common.

Rationale
This sweater is made from top quality cashmere in our factory in Italy. The result of this is that the sweater feels very soft and comfortable on the skin.

Question
How important is comfort for you?

Example Three

The customer is looking at our watches but is worried that we are not known for watches and is concerned about their reliability.

Acknowledge or thank
I can understand the point you raise

Rationale
Although our heritage is in clothing, we have been selling watches for the past five years. All our watches are made with Swiss movements and are of the highest quality. In addition they all come with a five-year warranty.

Question
How important is it for you to know they are backed by a long guarantee?

The more time front-line colleagues can identify the most common objections and become comfortable with applying the simple method above, the more likelihood they will improve their ability to deal with objections from customers.

Exercise

Ask the group to list the most common objections on specific products.

Once they have listed the objections, split the group into pairs and share the main objections out.

Each pair then has to apply the method from above and present this back for each objection to the rest of the group.

Chart all the objections on flipcharts around the wall with the solutions next to the corresponding objections.

Ask each person at random to give you the solution to a particular objection.

The more of this you do, the more comfortable your colleagues will become with this method.

The reality, however, is that whilst many customers do purchase, there are those that decide not to do so, despite you giving them a great experience, for one reason or another. It can often be difficult to remain upbeat, positive and motivated after experiencing several customers in succession deciding not to buy from you.

The internal dialogue that we referred to previously could easily, without us even realising it, go into overdrive with thoughts like:

- I think I'm losing my touch.
- I will never make my targets.
- They are just out browsing today.
- They have no money until the end of the month.

How much more helpful would it be to have the following thoughts or beliefs:

- We had a great conversation and I am sure she will come back again.
- Perhaps next time I will present slightly less options – I may have confused her.
- I should have closed the sale when I was sure of the buying signal.
- When I use my sales strategies effectively a sale will follow.
- I am sure the customer will go away with a positive image of our brand.

I'm sure you will agree that by having thoughts similar to those in this second list will ensure that we remain upbeat, positive and motivated and will therefore be able to engage positively with the next customer that comes along. The second list will serve us far better than the first.

The final point in this chapter is to be careful and aware of our assumptions:

Below is a transcript of a conversation between the captain of a US naval ship with Canadian authorities off the coast of Newfoundland in October 1995. This radio conversation was released by the Chief of Naval Operations on October 10 1995.

The captain of the US naval ship begins the conversation.

American captain: "Please divert your course 15 degrees to the North to avoid a collision."

Canadian authorities: "Recommend you divert your course 15 degrees to the South to avoid a collision."

American: “This is the captain of a US Navy ship. I say again, divert your course.”

Canadians: “No, I say again, you divert your course.”

American: “This is the aircraft carrier USS Abraham Lincoln, the second largest ship in the United States fleet. We are accompanied by three destroyers, three cruisers and numerous support vessels. I demand that you change your course 15 degrees north. That’s one five degrees north, or counter measures will be undertaken to ensure the safety of this ship.”

Canadians: “This is a lighthouse. Your call.”

The above is a great example of how our personal assumptions can be so off course.

So take time to build rapport with your customers and understand their needs. Work hard not to make assumptions because they can so often be wrong.

27

MAXIMISING SALES AT THE FITTING ROOM

The fitting room – where customers in a retail shop try on clothes – presents us with a great opportunity to maximise sales. Research tells us that 70% of those who try an item or items on in the fitting room, go on to make a purchase. It is therefore really important that we pay special attention to customers around the fitting room. My personal experience of how I have been treated at the fitting room has varied considerably. Often I will be shown to the fitting room and the assistant disappears. This then leaves it very difficult for me if I need another size. Other times the assistant will be too interested and will not leave me alone.

Here are some key guidelines I believe will help you achieve that service balance and maximise the sales opportunity.

Greet the customer – welcome them to the fitting room.

It is important to greet the customer as they approach the fitting room. It is important to make them feel as comfortable as possible, After all, they are about to take their clothes off in a public place.

Be attentive.

This does not mean get in the fitting room with them but there is nothing more frustrating when you go to try something on and it is either on the wrong size hanger or just does not fit well. It is unlikely that a customer will then spend time getting dressed, go and get another size to try, come back, get undressed and try it on again.

It makes sense therefore, when the customer first approaches the fitting room and you have greeted them, that you check that they have the correct size and make sure that you let them know that you will be close by if they need any further help.

Encourage them to show you.

We all love to get confirmation especially if we are on our own. Encourage your customers to come out and show you the item when they have it on. Remember to be honest. If you think there is something that would look better on them, say so in a diplomatic way. Then go and find an alternative.

Accessorise.

Think about what will go well with what they are trying on. Remember the importance of timing when you introduce it.

Make a positive comment.

Make them feel good about what they are buying by making a positive comment.

"That looks great" or "that goes really well together."

Summary of giving great service at the fitting room

1. Greet the customer.
2. Be attentive.
3. Encourage the customer to show you.
4. Accessorise.
5. Make a positive comment.

28

CLOSING THE SALE

Buying Signals

Before attempting to close the sale it is important to watch for buying signals. These are the signals that the customer gives off that let us know that they wish to go ahead and make the purchase. Now sometimes this can be really easy to spot, especially if the customer announces: "This is just the one – I know that she is going to love it! Thank you so much for your help – I think I will take this one." Or if a customer nods "Yes" to herself and says quietly "Perfect."

In many cases, however, it is not so clear and as we are not mind readers we have to listen and watch carefully for the signals. So let's explore when a buying signal is taking place. You will have experienced many examples I am sure but I have listed below a few of the most common ones.

If a customer:

- asks about other items that would work well with their original product,
- shows an interest in after-care methods or the warranty, or
- makes inquiries about the returns policy...

...close the sale!

Once you observe or hear a buying signal, it is vitally important to attempt to close the sale. If you wait too long the customer could change his or her mind and if you try too soon the customer could feel under pressure and then walk away without buying. There is no exact science here, instead one has to make a conscious decision based on what we have heard or observed. We may not get it right every time but if we listen carefully to how the customer responds to our suggestions and watch their facial expressions, we will begin to build our experience and confidence in this area.

When we do not get it right, do not be put off. Think of it this way, every time we get it wrong, we are one step closer to getting it right. Take professional sports people as an example, they train every day serving in tennis, taking shots at the goal in football, or throwing the ball at the basket in basket ball. They never make it 100% of the time. The more they practise, however, the better they become and you will too.

When we do decide to close the sale there are many different types of closing methods. In fact there has been much written on the subject of closing the sale. If we are not careful we can over-complicate things. So let's keep it simple and consider the following three types.

Direct close (this is a question asking directly for the business)

The direct close is a direct question that asks the customer for the sale.

"Would you like to go ahead with this one?"

"I think that you have made a great choice, would you like to buy this one?"

"Would you like to buy this one or that one?"

Assumptive close

The assumptive close assumes that the customer has decided to purchase, so the question is about something else – This one does take some confidence.

"How will you be paying?"

"Would you like me to gift-wrap this one?"

"Are you keeping this one on for today?"

"Did you just want the one, or are you going for both?"

The Need Method

Is there anything else you need?

When you ask the question above the customer will respond in one of two ways:

The customer will either say something along the lines of "No, I'm fine thanks with this." If they are still holding the product in their hands, you then know you have closed the sale.

The alternative is that they will say something like, "actually, do you do…?" You are then on to your next sale.

Sometimes with this technique, they will look up as if they are searching for something and sometimes they start with a "no" and then change to a "yes".

In this second response where they have asked you for something else, and you have got them the next item, simply ask the question again. "Is there anything else you need?"

We are not mind readers. We should keep asking this question until they say no.

A few years ago we were working with the retailer Past Times. It was coming up to the Christmas period when I received a call from one of their store managers. She came on the phone extremely excited and went on to explain how she used the close method "Is there anything else you need?" to the same customer five times until they said "no, thanks that's it for today."

When I asked her "did the customer ask her why she keeps asking the same question?" she replied "No, he just kept on asking for different items." Now remember that it was a gift retailer and it was during the lead up to Christmas, but it demonstrated just how powerful this technique can be.

The Alternative Strategy:

This can be assumptive too, but it can often be used to make the customer choose an item.

"Do you prefer the blue dial or the black one?"

"Is it fine as is, or shall I adjust it?"

"Which one can you see yourself wearing most, the blue stripe one or the gold one?"

It is important to note that, after asking whichever question you think is most appropriate for the situation, keep quiet and wait for the answer. It can feel a bit awkward as you become aware of the silence for a few seconds but this silence gives the customer a chance to make a decision. Try hard to resist the temptation to fill the silence for the customer. At this point in the sale you should have done all the talking that you needed to have done.

29

A GREAT LASTING IMPRESSION

This chapter addresses two issues: firstly why it is so important to leave your customer with a great lasting impression and secondly how to leave your customer with a great lasting impression. So why is it so important to leave your customers with a great lasting impression? In my opinion this relates to those customers who make a purchase as well as those who do not. It is interesting that many organisations are only interested in how much money they take on that particular, day, week or month. What I think is more important is the "lifetime value of a customer".

What do I mean by this? Consider you have an average customer who visits you four times a year and on average spends £100 each time they visit. That means they are worth £400 a year to you. If you then consider how many years they may shop with you over their lifetime, then you have calculated their lifetime value. In this particular case let's say that they may shop with you over a period of 25 years. This would mean that their lifetime value is £10,000.

It is therefore crucial that we do not see the customer to be worth the value of one visit i.e. £100, but instead we think of them to be worth a potential £10,000. Even if they do not purchase on this particular occasion, what is important is that they have a good experience, still feel valued by us and decide to come back again and again.

In addition, if a customer decides to make a purchase but as soon as we close the sale we move on to the next customer or we change our attitude towards them, the impression that they leave with would not be one that might encourage them to come back and shop with us in the future. It is therefore essential that every customer leaves with a great lasting impression where they feel valued and welcome any time.

So how can we leave our customers with a great lasting impression?

Very often you may serve someone on the shop floor but it is then not always possible for you to put their purchases through the till. The till operator then has the responsibility to process the purchase and leave the customer with a great lasting impression. Let's look at what we can do around the till operation, to leave your customers with a great lasting impression

Here's a guide to leaving your customers with a great lasting impression at the point of sale.

Thanks for waiting

If they've had to wait while you finish off a customer before them say thank you for waiting. We've all been standing in a queue at the checkout, tapping our foot and looking at our watch. When we get to the front of the queue the person says "thank you for waiting", what do we say? We say "that's OK!" It really helps to diffuse the situation and make us feel better about having to wait a short while.

Make a positive comment about the product they are purchasing

Although you haven't got time for a ten minute conversation with every customer, you do have time to make a positive comment to each customer. Sometimes customers talk themselves out of the purchase when queuing to pay, so it's really important to re-enforce what our customers have decided to buy.

This does not have to be complicated or long winded just something positive.

Examples of some simple positive comments:

- That's lovely or that looks great.
- That's really smart.
- I love that colour.
- That's part of our new range.
- They go really well together.
- I'm sure they will love it.

Pack carefully

When we make our final selection either from a rack or a shelf, I am sure you like to pick the one at the back or the one that looks in the most pristine condition. As we make our way to pay for our purchase very often we start to imagine ourselves either wearing it if it is a piece of clothing or using it around the house. In other words in our eyes we already own it. How do we then feel when we get to the till and it is just thrown into a bag?

I was recently in a retail store whose name I won't mention. I was queuing to pay. I noticed the assistant on the till when removing the hanger from the customers sweater, did so by removing it by the neck first. In doing so the tight crew neck became a loose V neck and the customer quite rightly said "I'm not having that now". I was totally on the side of the customer despite the fact that I then had to wait five minutes while we waited for a replacement to be found.

So make sure you fold and put the goods in the bag with care – they are now the customer's property and they don't want to see them stretched out of shape or thrown into the bag.

Parting statement

Finally hand the goods over to the customer and remember to thank them for their business.

A simple thank you, goodbye and we hope to see you again soon will ensure that this last part of the transaction is a memorable one.

In summary therefore, let's remember to give every customer a great experience at the end of the sale process whether they make a purchase or not. It makes a real difference to the impression every customer has as they leave your store and creates a much better chance of them choosing to shop with you in the future.

30

CHOOSE TO GO THE EXTRA MILE FOR YOUR CUSTOMER

The ideas and techniques contained within this second section are all tried and tested over many years of working face to face with customers in many different market places. For me however there is one more key thing I wish to share with you. This is the importance of going the extra mile for your customer.

Are we all customers? Of course we are. Most of us shop for something most days. Therefore we have a pretty good idea as to how we like to be treated in terms of service and how we definitely do not like to be treated in terms of service.

So if we think back to the better experiences that we have encountered and think about what it was about those experiences that made it special for us we will probably have encountered someone who was:

- Friendly.
- Helpful.
- Smiled and said hello.
- Went out of their way to help.
- Showed an interest in us personally.

Or perhaps it was that they simply went the extra mile. It's really interesting that I never find people say they have just had a great experience in a business because they got the seven stages of the sale delivered perfectly! It is invariably about how they were treated by a particular person.

If we consider this list for a moment and ask ourselves is there anything or anyone stopping us doing any of these in our business, the answer has to be no. No one in any sales organisation will be saying to their people don't be friendly, helpful, show an interest, etc. Of course they wouldn't be doing that. It wouldn't be great for business.

So why is it, we very often experience the opposite – unfriendly, unhelpful, no smile, no greeting, no interest shown etc.?

As I said earlier, we don't believe this is about training as we cannot train anyone to be friendly, helpful, welcoming, go out of their way or show an interest. We have to make that choice ourselves. The choice is a conscious decision of how we are every day when we come to work with our customers and each other.

So how can we go the extra mile for our customers and really WOW them so that they remember the experience, tell others and come back time after time.

The following stories are fantastic examples of where individuals have gone the extra mile. They have thought about their particular business and their roles within them and have really done something special for their customer. Not because they were told to but because they chose to do so.

How will you make your customers go WOW?

Example one – Johnny the Bagger

The following is a true story of one person who chose to go the extra mile and put his personal signature on the job which went on to inspire a whole organisation.

Barbara Glantz, a training consultant, was hired by a large supermarket chain to lead a customer service programme. She discussed how everyone can make a difference and create positive experiences for customers that would motivate them to keep coming back time and time again.

She asked everyone to think about something they could do for their customer that would make them feel special. She tasked everyone on the programme to do that.

A short time after she received a phone call from a nineteen-year-old assistant called Johnny. He went on to tell Barbara how he had liked what she had said. At first he said that he could not think of anything that would make his customers feel special as he just helped customers pack their bags. Then he had an idea.....

Every night after work he would come home and find a thought of the day. If he couldn't find one he would make one up. When Johnny had a good thought for the day he set it up on the computer and printed some copies. Johnny then cut out each quotation, signed his name on the back and brought them to work the next day. When he finished bagging someone's shopping he put his thought for the day in their bag and simply added "Thanks for shopping with us."

Johnny had not realised it at the time but what he had done was create special moments for all his customers. They all loved his quotations.

The manager of the store noticed when he was doing his morning inspection Johnny's queue was three times longer than anyone else's. Trying to open more tills to alleviate the queues no one would move. Customers just said it was OK. They wanted to be in Johnny's queue to get his thought for the day. Johnny was truly delighting his customers. Customers admitted that they were shopping there more often just to get Johnny's thought for the day.

As the months went by Johnny's idea of creating thoughts for the day transformed the store. Customers were talking about his store, coming back time after time and bringing their friends.

A wonderful spirit of service spread throughout the entire store and all because Johnny chose to make a difference. What Johnny had come up with was not necessarily rocket science but it was loving. It came from his heart. – It was real. That is what touched his customers and his peers in the store.

Great service comes from the heart.

Example two – Joshie the Giraffe

A family experienced the Ritz-Carlton hotel signature customer service in a way that will be talked about for many years to come. A family including two children spent a few days at the Ritz-Carlton hotel on Amelia Island (Florida). When they arrived home, they discovered that their son's beloved stuffed giraffe, named Joshie, had gone missing. As most parents know, children can become very attached to special blankets, teddy bears and the like. Their son was extremely fond of his Joshie, and was absolutely distraught when faced with the idea of going to sleep without his favourite friend. While trying to put him to bed the first night home, Joshie's father decided to tell a little white lie.

"Joshie is fine," he said. "He's just taking an extra long holiday at the Ritz Carlton." His son seemed to accept this little white lie, and was finally able to fall asleep, Joshie-less for the first time in a long while.

That very night, the Ritz-Carlton called to tell them they had found Joshie. Thankfully, he had been found, no worse for wear, in the laundry and was handed over to the hotel's loss prevention team. Joshie's dad admitted to the staff about the story he told his son and asked if they would mind taking a picture of Joshie on a lounge chair by the pool to substantiate his fabricated story. The loss prevention team agreed to do it, and he hung up the phone very relieved.

A couple days went by, and they received a package from the hotel. It was their son's Joshie, along with some Ritz-Carlton-branded "goodies" (a frisbee, football, etc.). Also included in the package was a photo album that meticulously documented his extended stay at the Ritz. It showed Joshie wearing shades by the pool, Joshie getting a massage at the spa, Joshie making friends (with other toys) and Joshie driving a golf cart on the beach. Joshie was even issued a Ritz-Carlton ID badge, made an honorary member of the Loss Prevention Team, and was allowed to help by taking a shift in front of the security monitors.

Needless to say, Joshie's parents were completely blown away by the Ritz-Carlton Loss Prevention Team. Their son, on the other hand, didn't care so much about the goodies and was just happy to have his Joshie back. They are sure however he'll have a greater appreciation for it when he grows up.

It goes without saying that the Ritz-Carlton can count on this family to be lifetime customers. But what they have created here is an experience so amazing that someone can't help but tell others about it as Joshie's family have done on many occasions and as I am doing so with you.

Example three – Creating Fans – Metro Bank

Metro Bank is committed to giving great service and going the extra mile for their customers.

Once when they had a processing problem with Mastercard, it came to their attention that a customer was having problems paying for their airline flights. A team member stepped in and put the customer's flights on her personal credit card so the customer could take advantage of the good deal that was being offered at the time.

On another occasion their IT system crashed and the call centre was unable to access customer accounts or details. At the same time a customer called and wanted to transfer funds from one account to his current account. He explained it was extremely urgent as he needed to pay a bill in the morning. A team member promised the customer that the payment would be made and said he would call him back as soon as the issue was resolved and the payment was made.

An hour later he called the customer to say the issue was still not resolved but he would stay in the office until the system was back up. It was finally fixed later that evening but not until after 11pm. He contacted the customer the following morning to make sure he was able to withdraw his funds. The customer made a point in letting the bank know how impressed he was that the team member had stayed on until the system was back up and he was able to complete the urgent transaction.

I was fortunate to attend a presentation given by Chris Brindley, the UK Managing Director of Metro Bank. Chris talked about ways to amaze customers. It all sounded very good so I decided I would go and check it out. I have to say I was very impressed in both the branches that I visited. Those that engaged with me did everything they could to help me. Nothing was too much trouble and I got the sense that the service culture he talked about creating was in fact touching all parts of the organisation.

I went to visit Chris in their head quarters at Holborn in London and again was impressed with the service. On arriving, Chris asked if I would like a tour of the bank and I accepted his kind offer. My immediate thought was that I would meet back up with Chris in his office after the tour. How wrong I was. Instead Chris personally took me around the bank and showed me all the different elements of the bank he was most proud of. In addition while Chris was showing me around he picked up pieces of paper from the floor and refilled leaflets that had run out.

This demonstrated to me that the service culture was not just talked about by the senior leaders within the organisation but was endemic throughout the organisation. What the leadership team within Metro Bank are doing that so many other organisations fail to do was role model the service behaviours that they wished to see on the front line of the bank's operations. In doing so they have created a culture that truly lives their customer first.

Well done Metro Bank – you have my vote!

PART TWO – QUIZ

1. **Why should we greet a customer?**

Answer: It helps the customer to feel comfortable.

2. **How do we greet the customer?**

Answer: Greet, make eye contact and smile.

3. **Why do we hold eye contact?**

Answer: To get a response. The response can tell us whether the customer is ok or not ok at that point.

4. **What are the two different types of 'responses'?**

Answer 1: The customer gives us good eye contact back, says hello then moves eye contact away again, quickly.

Answer 2: The customer gives us good eye contact back, says hello, then continues to hold eye contact but says no more.

5. **When should we approach a customer?**

Answer: When they give off an approach signal.

6. **Give one example of an approach signal?**

Answer: When the customer is looking round confused.

7. **How should we approach?**

Answer: After first observing the approach signal, approach the customer from the side within their line of sight and at about 6-8ft away from them.

8. **What are the four types of questions discussed and what does each one do?**

Answer:

- Open – opens up the conversation and reveals thoughts opinions and feelings.
- Closed – closes down the conversation.
- Probing – gets you more information.
- Testing Understanding – ensures you have the correct information.

9. **How can you ensure that you are listening effectively?**

Answer: Make eye contact, repeat back to demonstrate listening, ask questions.

10. **Why are feelings important within features and benefits?**

Answer: Feelings weigh more heavily on the decision scales.

11. **What do we mean by link sales?**

Answer: It's where you introduce an additional item or accessory to the customer that will complement / add value to their original item.

12. **How can we deal with objections?**

Answer: Use the PRQ strategy. Praise the customers comment, give the rationale, ask a leading question.

13. **How can we close the sale?**

Answer:

- Direct close "Would you like to go ahead with this one?"
- Assumptive close "How will you be paying?"
- NEED Method "Was there anything else you need today?"

14. **How can we leave the customer with a great lasting impression?**

Answer:

- Greet nicely.
- Thank them for waiting if they have had to wait.
- Make a positive comment.
- Pack considerately.
- Positive parting comment.

PART THREE

SUSTAINING THE MOMENTUM

EQUIPPING YOUR TEAM TO STAY "FIRED UP AND READY TO GO"

31

INTRODUCTION

Equipping your team to stay "fired up and ready to go" has always been the hardest stage of creating and maintaining a great customer experience in any organisation. Priorities are constantly changing, and as soon as one initiative has been completed there is usually another one about to start. In addition, the fact that people's mobility is much greater these days just adds to the ever changing set of new priorities. The reality, however, is that the customer has always got to be the first priority but grinding that priority into reality I suppose is where the real hard work starts.

I'd like to begin therefore by stressing that your role as a manager, director or business owner, is absolutely crucial to getting and then keeping your team fired up and ready to go. If you believe that Part One and Two of this book can help you and your teams engage more effectively with your customers and each other, then in my view you have absolute influence over sustaining the momentum created by the first two parts.

If having read Part Three, you and your management team all commit to leading by example, coaching your teams on a regular basis and ensuring the other factors outlined are put into practise, then you will keep your team fired up and ready to go and continue to live your customer first.

Organisations that are truly committed to driving a customer centric culture understand that sheep dipping teams through customer centred workshops is just the start of the change needed. The way that management at all levels behave and the use of coaching plays a major role in sustaining any momentum. If they role model the desired behaviours and have coaching conversations with their staff on a regular basis, then we often witness behavioural change that is sustained over time. Where the above is missing, it rarely makes any difference at all.

32

SET CLEAR EXPECTATIONS / REPORT BACK ON PERFORMANCE

To begin with, it is really important that all members of staff in whatever role they have within your business, are clear on what is expected of them. As a manager therefore it's critical to ensure that everyone is informed of what is expected of them. It surprises me how often I go into organisations, speak to employees at all levels and they comment about the fact that their line manager does not tell them what they want or expect from them. My advice to you here is quite simple.

"Don't be that manager!"

A well documented method for ensuring team members are clear on what is expected of them is to set SMART objectives together. This ensures that you are both clear on the expectations from the outset. Once these objectives have been set, make sure that you schedule in time to review them on a regular basis. Once they have been achieved, sit down again and set some new ones.

For those of you who are not familiar with SMART objectives, in simplistic terms, make sure when you are setting objectives you can answer "yes" to the following questions: If the answer is "no" or you are not really sure then go back and redefine the objective.

- **S**PECIFIC – Is the objective specific?
- **M**EASURABLE – Is the objective measurable? How can we measure the success?

- **A**CHIEVABLE – Is the objective achievable?
- **R**ELEVANT – Is the objective relevant to the business overall objective/s?
- **T**IMEBOUND – Does the objective have a timeline, when does it have to be done by?

Reflect on and discuss performance

Once everyone in the team is clear on what is expected of them, it is equally important to ensure that they are aware of how they are doing compared to those expectations. This is relevant on a personal level and for their particular role. Reporting back on performance against expectations plays a major part in the motivation and therefore performance of your individual team members.

Performance reviews should not only take place once or twice a year, but instead should be held on a regular basis. The more regular, open and honest dialogue about performance that takes place between a member of staff and their line manager, the more chance you have of ensuring the desired behaviours are taking place in the first place and continue to take place.

33

ROLE MODEL DESIRED BEHAVIOURS

One of the most powerful ways to ensure your teams behave with your customers and each other in a way that you want them to behave is by role modelling those behaviours yourself.

When working with a Hospital Foundation Trust, I was faced with a dilemma that the board recognised the importance of treating patients like customers but they were not demonstrating those desired behaviours with their employees. As a result it was no surprise to me that, despite putting the whole workforce through a customer centric transformation programme, behaviours remained the same.

Eventually the Chief Executive, who was committed to driving a service culture, finally understood that in order to really change behaviour within the trust, the Board needed to change their behaviour first. Over time they did this and over time the behaviours across the organisation began to change. Do not be under any illusion. This does take time, but in my opinion no matter what you do, the behaviours need to be led from the top.

Richard Wolff, former Retail and International Director of Marks and Spencer, Julia Brown former Chief Operating Officer of Enfield Primary Care Trust, Vic de Chuna the current Chief Executive of The Curo Housing Group and Chris Brindley Managing Director of The Metro Bank UK, are all living examples of how role modelling the behaviours you want to see demonstrated by your teams are demonstrated on a daily basis by themselves.

34

BARRIERS THAT PREVENT THE TEAM BEING "FIRED UP AND READY TO GO"

"Things that matter most should never be at the mercy of things that matter least."
Stephen Covey

So what barriers exist that prevent us from ensuring our team are "fired up and ready to go" in order to engage positively with our customers?

Exercise – Barriers

I would now like you to think about and make a note of all the barriers that will either prevent you from engaging with your customers yourself as the leader, or coaching your teams to engage positively with your customers. Take time to really think about all the barriers you can. It's really important to list them all and be careful that we do not brush any under the carpet.

List of barriers

-
-
-
-
-
-

-
-
-
-
-
-
-
-
-
-
-
-
-
-

Now I'd like you to read the following quotation and the question that follows it:

"Things that matter most should never be at the mercy of things that matter least"
Stephen Covey

If we have agreed that the customer must be our number one priority i.e. the thing that matters most, then where are your customers when all these barriers are getting in the way and preventing us from living our customer first?

It is at this point that everyone realises that it is easier said than done.

Circle of Influence

So to help us deal with all these barriers let me introduce you to a model called the "Circle of Influence" created by Stephen Covey. The "Circle of Influence" is a useful model to help us deal with the barriers. Let me explain how the model works:

The Circle of Influence

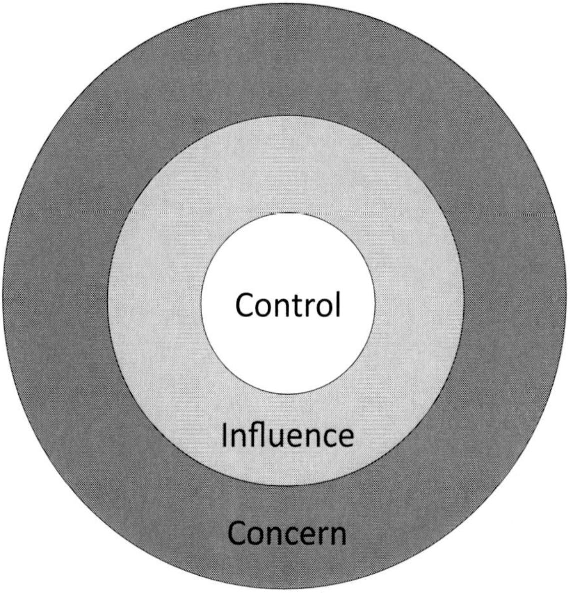

Here we have a series of circles. In the outer circle we have what we call the "Circle of Concern".

Now, everyone has a wide range of concerns – it may be our health, our children, the weather, problems at work, problems at home, crime etc. – some of which we have control and influence over, some of which we don't. For example I may be concerned that it is going to rain later today. As I have no influence or control over the weather, this would sit within the sphere of concern.

Now, moving inwards, we have the "Circle of Influence". Some concerns will sit within this "Circle of Influence" as we may be able to influence them. For example I may be concerned whether or not you are going to take on board and put into practise the ideas I am sharing with you. Now, provided I have presented them in a way that makes sense to you there is a chance that at the very least you may try them out. This concern therefore, would sit within the sphere of influence.

Another example of a concern that would sit within the sphere of influence may be around which party or coalition of parties will win the next general election and go on to run the country. As we live in a democracy and all have the opportunity to vote, we can influence the decision with our vote. The concern therefore would sit within our sphere of influence.

And, moving inwards again, we have the “Circle of Control”. This contains concerns that we have total control over. For example I may be concerned that I have put on a few pounds over the last few months. Clearly I have control over this as I decide how much I eat and how often I take exercise. So you can see how this concern would sit in the inner circle, the circle of control.

Covey talks about proactive people and reactive people. He claims that proactive people go to work on their concerns that sit within their ‘Sphere of Influence and Control’ and by doing so, their ability to influence and control increases. I suppose it’s similar to a muscle – the more we work a muscle the bigger and stronger it gets.

Reactive people on the other hand spend time worrying, moaning about and complaining about the concerns they have that they have little or no influence or control over. As a result of doing this their Circle of Concern gets bigger, due to the muscle effect again, while their Circle of Influence and Circle of Control get smaller. In other words their ability to influence and their ability to control reduces. If we do not use a muscle it reduces in size.

Exercise continued

I would like you now to revisit your list of barriers that will either prevent you from engaging with your customers or coaching your teams to engage effectively with your customers and decide which of them are actually within your “Circle of Control or Circle of Influence”.

When you have decided, put a tick next to those you feel you have some control / influence over and leave the rest blank. If you have the slightest influence or the slightest control you must give it a tick. But be prepared to justify why you believe you have or do not have any influence or control over certain barriers.

When we run this activity with groups of managers, although there are usually plenty of perceived barriers that first appear on the list, it does not take long, when mapping Covey's model the "Sphere of Influence and Control" onto them, to realise that in the vast majority of cases they do in fact have some degree of influence and control over them.

It is very rare that I come across a group that argues they have influence over less than 85% of the barriers. On the rare occasion that I do, I always encourage the others in the group who believe they do have influence and control, to share with the rest of the group why they believe they can influence and control the individual barriers. In the majority of cases the end result is that the other members of the group are persuaded by these members that they do indeed have influence over the vast majority of the perceived barriers.

Once we have reached this point, we are ready to move on. Until this point, it becomes very difficult to have managers take on board the next stages if they still believe no matter what, they cannot keep it alive or sustained due to the barriers.

35

COACHING

So once we have it clear in our heads and our hearts that, despite the fact that barriers exist, we do have influence and control over them, we are now ready to move on to the importance of and how to coach our teams.

Let's begin with explaining why coaching is so important in driving behaviours or in this case supporting our teams to engage effectively with our customers.

Sigmund Freud's 'Iceberg Model of Consciousness' explains that our conscious behaviour is only the visible 10% of our psyche i.e. the tip of the iceberg. The deeper motivators of our behaviours – equating to 90% of our mental nature – lie submerged in our sub-conscious or unconscious mind.

These deeper motivators include our feelings, thoughts, values, beliefs, confidence and attitude. It's only when we have regular coaching conversations with our teams that we truly build staff confidence and truly get to know what they are thinking and how they are feeling. When we know this, we have a much greater chance of affecting the desired behavioural change.

So let's now explore what exactly do we mean by coaching?

Exercise – Coaching

What comes to mind when I say the word "coaching" to you?

-
-
-
-
-
-

"Instruct or train somebody" (The Oxford Dictionary)

I prefer the following definitions:

- ***"Unlocking a person's potential to maximise their own performance."***
- ***"A form of helping them to learn for themselves rather than teaching, telling or instructing them."***

If that is what coaching is, what do you think are good qualities of a successful coach?

Exercise

Think back to a time when someone coached you really well. It could for example have been a school sport, when you learnt to drive or when you learnt a new role or task at work. When you have recalled that time, I want you to think about the person and think about what was it that they did specifically that made you recall them as a great coach?

Qualities of a successful coach

-
-
-
-
-
-

Usual answers:

Good observer, good listener, supportive, was always encouraging, patient, showed interest, attentive, challenges, pushes me out of my comfort zone, encourages me to come up with the solution and sets realistic objectives.

Let's imagine now that we have asked all of your members of staff, who report directly to you, to come into this room and I then ask them to describe you, their manager. How many of them do you think would describe you using the same words as those written above i.e. the words that describe a great coach?

No need to answer that out loud, but just consider it. Coaching does not have to be and is not complicated. If we want to be a great coach all we need to do is make sure we are behaving in the way described above. After all these were the qualities that you thought about and why you remembered the people that you recalled.

So, if that is what coaching is, and those are the qualities we feel a great coach should possess then how should we go about coaching?

If I were to say to you that you had to coach three people in your team before noon tomorrow, how would you go about that?

The Energize Coaching Model

When we first developed the engagement behaviours back in 2000, we noticed that the managers that were role modelling the behaviours themselves and having coaching conversations on the shop floor with their team members, saw the biggest increase in sales and conversion and were able to sustain those sales levels.

We realised we had to ensure that all the managers understood the need for coaching and were able to do so. So we went to work on identifying what were the conversations that were making the biggest difference. The Energize coaching model was then born.

I make no apologies for it appearing a pretty simple model. I truly believe the simplicity makes it effective because everyone can remember it and it's easy to use. Try and google coaching and you could spend years reading all the different models and theories available. I think what we discovered were tried and tested questions, put together in a simple model, that will enable you to coach.

An important point to raise is that it is equally important to coach team members when you have witnessed them behaving in a desirable way as well as a non desirable way. The motivating factor of catching someone doing something right and being recognised for it is huge.

Think about it for one minute. Try and recall a time when you last had a positive conversation about your performance with your line manager. I am sure that feeling was really powerful and propelled you to keep behaving and therefore operating at that level. But what happens to that great feeling over a period of time? Yes, it fades, just as a balloon when blown up and left for a while deflates. So, how are you going to get that feeling back again? Yes, that's right you have to get praised again. How are you going to get praised again? By behaving in that same way again. So remember coaching conversations involving praise are equally important and hugely motivational.

Step One – Observe

Observe what's happening. It is really important that you have observed an interaction with the member of staff and the customer before you can contemplate having a coaching conversation with them.

That does not mean you go up to them and say something like "I'm going to observe you and then give you some feedback or some coaching" I am sure that they would feel a little intimidated if you were to take that approach. Instead, just observe them as you are going about your usual tasks and activities.

Step Two – Ask how it went?

Asking questions around how the sale or interaction with the customer went, will enable the person you are coaching to start talking about and reflecting upon what had just happened.

For example:

- Tell me about that last sale.
- Talk me through that sale you've just had, where the lady purchased that skirt.
- How did it go with that customer who has just left the store?

At this point allow the member of staff to give you their version of the events that you just witnessed. It is so much more powerful when you ask someone else for their opinion and their thoughts before you start to share your own. Let's be honest, in most cases we all know if we have had a good or a bad interaction. They are then much more willing to get involved, to take part or to listen to what you have to say. So listen to their point of view first.

"Seek first to understand then be understood"

Stephen Covey

Step Three – Ask how it could be done differently?

Next get them to reflect on "If there was anything they would do differently next time."

For example:

- How could you do it differently?
- How might you change your approach next time?
- What do you feel you could have improved upon?

These are really powerful questions. When you ask these questions, the person begins to coach themselves and you have become the facilitator. Again, if the member of staff comes up with ideas for an improved approach themselves, they are much more likely to put them into practice than if they are just told what to do differently.

Step Four – Make suggestions

Now that does not mean that you should not make any suggestions, but it is really important to allow the person you are coaching the opportunity to come up with the solution or suggestions themselves in the first place. If they cannot think of what they could do differently to improve or they do not talk about what you think they should do to make an improvement, then at this point it is perfectly fine to make some suggestions yourself. There is a much greater chance that they will take on board your ideas at this point simply because they have had a chance to air their views.

For example:

- Perhaps you could try just greeting the customer.

- Why don't you think about the link sale to go with the product and suggest it to the customer?
- Maybe you could watch for more definite buying signals before you close the sale.

Step Five – Lead by example

Always ensure that whatever you ask your team to do, you can, or are prepared to do yourself.

There is nothing more powerful than the manager role modelling behaviours that he/she wants to see displayed within his/her team. For many people seeing the desired behaviours is often a very effective way to help front-line teams fully understand what you want them to do and the way in which you would like them to behave.

Coaching exercise

The only way to get coaching going in your business/organisation is to get out there and start having coaching conversations. So take a look at the following situations and think about how you can use the coaching model described above to start the conversation:

Example One

You observe a very keen member of staff repeatedly go up to customers and ask if they need any help. But the staff member is constantly being rebuffed by those customers and you can see the staff member's confidence level dropping.

You know that if they just said hello and smiled they would have a much better chance of the customer engaging back in a positive way. What conversation do you have with them to ensure that it does not just become a monologue of what they should do differently?

Answer:

You ask the member of staff:

- *How they are finding greeting the customers? How is it working?*
- *Is there anything they think they could usefully try that may prevent them getting repeatedly rebuffed?*

If they come up with the solution that you have in mind – great, if they do not then at this point it is fine to make a suggestion:

- *Why don't you try just saying hello to them and smile?*

Finally, remember to lead by example and demonstrate what you would like them to do.

Example two

You observe a member of staff who has been with you a while making lots of single item sales. She fails to introduce other products that you sell and which would certainly enhance and complement what her customers are buying.

Answer:

You ask the member of staff:

- *How are your link sales going?*
- *How could you introduce other lines that will compliment the ones they are buying?*
- *What could you ask them that may help increase the number of items they buy?*

Again, If they come up with the solution that you have in mind – great, if they do not then at this point it is fine to make a few suggestions:

- *Suggest another product that you think would go well with what they are about to buy.*

Finally, remember to lead by example and demonstrate what you would do.

Coaching quotations

1. *"Give a man a fish and you feed him for a day, teach him to fish and you feed him for life."* (Ancient Chinese proverb)

2. *"Any job has excitement in it, if you have excitement in you!"* (Unattributed)

3. *"Things that matter most, must never be at the mercy of those which matter least."* (Stephen Covey)

4. *"The one who listens does the most work, not the one who speaks!"* (Stephen Covey)

5. *"The key to listening is with the eyes and the heart."* (Stephen Covey)

6. *"If you think you can or you think you cannot you are right."* (Eleanor Roosevelt)

36

LISTEN TO WHAT YOUR CUSTOMERS ARE SAYING

"Seek first to understand and then be understood."
Stephen Covey

During my early years working in retail, while I was working for Marks and Spencer in the London Marble Arch flagship branch, I used to spend a large part of my time with directors, executives and head office buyers who would appear unannounced daily and want to know what customers were buying and why, and what they weren't buying and why.

They would talk to customers and find out from them what they thought of particular products. In those days Marble Arch store was a test bed for all new lines. Everything started in the flagship store. Marble Arch store alone represented a significantly high percentage of the overall sales for each department and so the buying teams could work out from just a few hours' sale in this store what level of buys they needed to commit to in advance for the whole business. They not only relied on the figures, they were keen to understand what customers thought and what they were saying to us. In many ways we became their eyes and ears.

Everyone from the chairman to the trainee buyers would visit the store regularly. In the chairman's case he would visit once a week to confirm that what he was being told at the head quarters was the same picture on the front line. Sometimes, he would bring executives and buyers with him and insist they explained why he was not seeing what they had told him in their meetings.

In his book *The Seven Habits of Highly Effective People*, Stephen Covey dedicates one of the seven habits to the importance of listening first and talking second. We have two ears and one mouth and we should use them in that proportion. This not only helps you to understand the person you are listening to better but it goes a long way to helping to build rapport and helping to build strong relationships.

The impact at a personal level is clear to everyone but it can also have a major impact on your business too. There is no better way to sustain a strong healthy business than making sure that you listen to what your customers are saying. And there is no better way to listen to what your customers are saying than to talk to them on a regular basis on your front line. Clearly Marks and Spencer had the right ideas in the nineties. Perhaps they have lost their way and have stopped listening to their customers since then as they have faced more challenging times.

These days we can capture customers' feedback through various channels. These channels are not mutually exclusive and my intention is to describe some of the most commonly used approaches. Whilst there are many routes these days to hear and read about what your customers think of your business, the traditional route of hearing it in real time on the shop floor is still vitally important. Online retail may be growing at a rapid pace but the vast majority of most retail business's sales are still taken from their bricks and mortar shops. So spend time in your stores, boutiques, call centres, hospital wards, ticket offices and you will hear first hand about what your customers think of your business.

In addition to listening to your customers, listen to what your front-line teams are saying. Many of our clients do this as they firmly believe it provides a collective view of what customers are saying.

Many organisations hold colleague consultation groups to understand how colleagues are feeling but also what customers are saying. Again these can be really useful in understanding what your customers are saying. National organisations hold these groups locally and nationally enabling them to understand which issues are local, regional or national.

Written feedback from customers

Some customers like to reflect and then write in with their comments. If they take the time to do this, they clearly feel quite strongly about their experience. It is therefore really important that you read carefully what your customers are saying and then respond to either thank them for the feedback or to inform them of how you intend to rectify it.

We all know from personal experience that we are quite forgiving if our complaint is dealt with satisfactorily. If our issue is dealt with well, we become brand ambassadors and share our story with other people. This has to be the best form of advertising for any company as, if you think about it, it's free. If on the other hand a letter or complaint is not dealt with well, the story is again shared with lots of our friends and colleagues, but in most cases it is blown up and is described much worse than the reality.

We have recently been working with a famous food business who have got frustrated when they made it easier for customers to complain to them, using social media. In the past sending feedback took a lot of effort, so people would only do that if the problem had made a significant impact on them and a solution was required. Now that it has become easier, customers will also complain about minor frustrations – the sort of stuff that they would previously not have mentioned, but that would influence future purchase decisions and they might have mentioned it to their friends.

So bringing these minor issues to the surface was a major improvement for the business concerned. They now had the opportunity to turn around issues that had lost them custom. Yet instead of being delighted, staff at their head office were frustrated as they now had to deal with (in their eyes) trivial complaints!

Due to the ability to feedback electronically and now via phone apps, the volume of feedback has increased significantly in recent years. Whilst this may mean a greater volume of work, ignore this at your peril. Remember if a customer has bothered to communicate with you, it is because they care.

"Your most unhappy customers are your greatest source of learning."

Bill Gates – Microsoft

If no-one tells you what is wrong or what they don't like, a business will keep doing what it is doing thinking that everything is OK. This can be lethal for any business. So it is far better to find out what is wrong while you have time to put it right.

Customer Focus Groups

Running customer focus groups can be an effective method to ascertain what your customers are thinking and how they feel about your business. They can be really insightful as to what extent they are experiencing good customer service or that you are satisfying their needs.

Careful planning is needed in setting these up and ensuring that:

1. You have a good cross section of your customer base.
2. You are clear on what you are trying to achieve and construct the questions accordingly.

You may find that you have to incentivise your customers to come along and pay their expenses etc.

Surveys

Customer surveys can also be useful in understanding what they think of the customer experience they receive. These need to be quick to complete, with carefully crafted questions around the key areas you wish to better understand.

Conclusion

Whatever insight you gain from either talking to customers on the front line, reading their written feedback or running customer focus groups and surveys, make sure that you take the necessary action that you believe will help to ensure that your teams continue to give your customers a great experience.

In a market place where many retailers are currently struggling, whilst others are growing and building market share at the expense of the struggling ones, it is clear to me that customer feedback is now as important as ever, so you ignore customers' niggles at your peril.

37

"WHAT GETS MEASURED GETS DONE"

"What gets measured gets done"
Tom Peters

"What gets measured gets improved"
Robin Sharma

I strongly believe there is truth in both the quotations above. Most of the organisations I have been involved with and support, talk about how they need to measure their performance in customer experience. Less however, actually put into place the relevant tools and processes to do so. Those that do think about and agree their measurement strategy prior to any work in this area do see tangible benefits.

In the old days car engines used to be prone to overheating. So car manufacturers installed equipment in cars to measure the oil and water temperature. The driver could then keep an eye on the state of the engine and adjust their driving behaviour as appropriate. Nowadays engine cooling has improved so much that most dashboards no longer show water temperature, and most drivers don't even think about it anymore.

What is clearly visible still on a dashboard is your speed. How many of us would exceed the speed limit if this was not clearly marked on the dashboard? So you could argue that measuring speed helps to keep us driving legally and prevents us from driving too fast in potentially dangerous conditions.

So, having a visible noticeboard highlighting how you are

performing, keeps everybody on track and motivated to achieve the overall goals or targets. It needs to be updated regularly so that teams remain interested, otherwise it will just blend in with the wall paper. Visual management, showing the metrics you decide are the important ones for your organisation, will help to keep everyone informed on what it is the team is aiming to achieve.

There are many ways of measuring customer experience and there are just as many ways to interpret the data once you get it back. My advice in this area therefore is to keep it simple and ensure those that interpret the data collected fully understand what you are trying to achieve.

Above all, if you believe that giving your customers a great experience will mean that they will purchase more and more often, then the key metric that you should always have your eye on is overall sales.

In addition, the metrics that can be directly influenced and therefore measured in a store environment and by front-line teams are the levels of conversion, average spend and units per transaction.

How well your teams engage with customers when they enter your business and how well they perform during the customer journey is totally in their hands and within their sphere of influence. It is really important therefore that everyone within the team understands how they can influence the important outcomes. The classic example here is the NASA cleaner, who, while holding the door open for a visitor of the space centre, replied to the question requesting what his role was by saying "I help to put men on the moon". There was no doubt in this cleaner's mind of what the key outcome was that they were all working towards. And, if you think about it, he was telling the truth.

At the same time, the manager needs to give licence to front-line staff to decide how they interact with customers so that they are doing the right thing for the customer.

It is important when planning an intervention to improve the customer experience that measurement takes place for a period of time prior to any activity or intervention. This then gives you a base-line figure to work from. Measurement should continue throughout the period that the intervention takes place and then for a period of time afterwards. By doing so you should not only be clear on the base line metric, you will also get a view of the initial impact of any intervention be it training, marketing or promotion as well as the impact once the activity has ended. Having clarity on post-implementation activity will allow you to measure how effective you are at launching and sustaining the initial intervention.

In addition, consider setting up a control group with areas of your business that are not involved with any of the intervention or activity. This is important as by comparing the trial group with the control group you will establish an accurate measurement of the impact of the intervention itself and not any external market factors i.e. general uplift in trade.

Conversion, average spend and units per transaction are familiar and easily understood by your front-line teams. They appreciate how they can impact them and the technology these days allows us to monitor and measure them at an individual level.

Mystery shopper

Mystery shopping is a popular independent measuring tool that many organisations favour. Ensuring the mystery shopping company understands accurately the behaviours you are trying to instil and then briefs their shoppers accordingly is critical. There is, for example, little point in the mystery shopper basing an assessment on how long it took until they were approached, if your business is quite rightly training your front-line teams to only approach when the customer gives off approach signals. This will only create frustration for your teams and risk them not utilising the training intervention.

Be careful that your front-line teams do not become obsessed with the mystery shopper and try to identify them. In this case, once they have visited for the month, giving great service can often go out of the window. Remember, mystery shopping is a snapshot measure and not something to get hung up on. What is important, is ensuring every customer that visits you, should receive great service.

In recent years, video mystery shopping has become popular. It does take away any excuses or denials that are often associated with the traditional methods. As it is much more expensive per visit, my advice is to use it as a tool on a small scale to demonstrate the reality to the rest of your business.

Net Promoter Score

Another recent and popular mechanism to measure customer and employee engagement is the net promoter score. Whether you have customers, patients or employees, your Net Promoter Score gives you a quick way to get feedback by asking the ultimate question:

> *"How likely is it that you would recommend this company to a friend or colleague?"*

If you've seen this question before, you're familiar with an easy and fast way to measure customer loyalty to your company, product, service, or brand.

This Net Promoter Score questionnaire gets you the data you need to quickly understand what customers feel about your organisation—and to react to any feedback both positive and negative. It also provides a commentary as to why they feel that particular way or what made them feel like that. A NPS score also makes it easy to set both internal performance benchmarks, as well as external benchmarks to compare against competitors in your industry.

Employee engagement

As discussed in the previous chapter, we understand that there is a direct relationship between how your staff feel about the business and the brand and how they then treat your customers. We are basically talking about the relationship between motivation of your workforce and sales performance.

Measuring how your employees feel about your organisation therefore should give you some rich insight as to how they are likely to treat your customers. If you need them to treat your customers better, then improving your employee engagement scores should help to do so. Many of our clients often run workshops to understand how employees feel and why. These are run alongside the manager's own instinct who may not be right or at least might not understand the 'why'.

So to conclude this section on measurement, I'm sure you will agree that there are quite a few things to think about. The first thing is to think through what you are trying to achieve. Then think about how you can measure the things you wish to achieve. Thirdly, put in place the mechanisms that will best measure them and finally continue to review the measurement on a regular basis and communicate your findings to the relevant personnel and take action accordingly before you set off again to re-measure.

38

RECRUITING THE RIGHT ATTITUDE

"Recruit for attitude and train for skill"

What do companies like Pret a Manger, Southwest Airlines and Ritz-Carlton have in common? They hire for attitude and train for skill. It's a simple idea, but one that has a major impact on how to successfully recruit and select new employees.

During their hiring process, these companies weigh 'attitudinal' characteristics very heavily. These are personal attributes that it's difficult to train employees on, such as being a positive person, having an upbeat personality, or possessing a keen ability to learn new things.

While these companies won't ignore technical skills, (Southwest doesn't put unqualified pilots in the cockpit, no matter how bright and positive they are) they nonetheless look very carefully at these other skills. By focusing on attitudinal characteristics that align with their company brand and values, these companies reinforce their culture with each new employee. And because they're hiring people whose values align with that culture, the end result is a workforce that's happier, more engaged and less likely to leave.

But the benefits of this hiring process do not stop there. When a team really lives the company brand, think how Southwest employees exude "fun", it differentiates the customer experience where it counts most – in customers' one-on-one interactions with your staff.

I first encountered the "recruit for attitude and train for skill" phrase when I was supporting Marks and Spencer in 2001. We had just delivered a large scale campaign across their store and head office network and I was asked to ensure that their recruitment process was aligned to the campaign we had delivered. We went to work to ensure that the right attitude was being assessed at interview stage.

As I mentioned, our customer engagement programmes explore in great detail the whole issue of attitude, how you choose your own attitude and how your attitude makes such a difference. You may have all the technical skills required for the job but if your attitude is wrong it's not going to build great relationships with your customers or allow a potential future employee to integrate well with the current team and ultimately be successful and progress within the business.

According to The Advanced Learner's Dictionary of Current English – attitude is defined as "a way of looking at life; a way of thinking, feeling or behaving". Attitude is therefore not just the way we think, but the way we feel and what we do.

Great organisations employ and engage great people. But how do we know great people when we see them? This is something with which organisations from different market places continue to wrestle and it's fair to say that ultimately it's not what the individual knows but more importantly that they have the right mind-set. The best predictor of future behaviour is past behaviour. Your personality does not change and essentially stays the same throughout your life. So during the recruitment process we need take time to consider what a candidate has done and achieved before – specifically in terms of attitudinal behaviour.

How to hire for attitude

So how should you go about hiring for attitude, filling your workforce with true brand ambassadors? Fortunately, there are approaches you can employ to do this. Here are some simple ways to hire for attitude:

1) Define clearly what you're looking for:

This principle revolves around the idea that the best way to hire people who will fit the organisational culture is to look at those individuals who are already successful within the organisation, identify the characteristics which make them successful and then to hire individuals with similar characteristics. Think about using personality profiling tools such as DISC or MBTI which will provide more clues about the individual's motivators and behaviours.

2) Be clear about expectations:

Take advantage of candidate self-selection by clearly broadcasting what qualities you look for when bringing on new staff. For example, if you tell the market that you are looking for extroverts – fewer introverts will apply and that's a good outcome for you and them. By defining what personal qualities you're searching for up-front, you make it more likely that candidates with those attributes will apply in the first place.

Work to tailor the job profile or advert to emphasise the positive attitude you're looking for. Be creative in describing the types of candidates you are looking for so the position and the company stands out from the crowd to the right candidates.

3) During the interview:

On the basis that past performance predicts future behaviour and reveals attitude, use competency based questions. Some common examples appropriate to most industry sectors include:

- Tell me about a time when you went beyond the call of duty to deliver an outstanding customer experience.
- Give me an example of how you respond to difficult co-workers.
- When did you last try something new when there was no guarantee of success?
- Tell me about the last serious mistake you made with a customer or colleague and how you reacted to it.

4) Involve employees in the hiring process:

Organisations who use employees to assess potential employees are utilising one of their most important assets. People who participate in the selection process are committed to helping the new recruit succeed and they are just as eager to make the right decision because they will be working alongside the new recruit.

When I worked with Pret a Manger in the UK, this was exactly what they did. Staff at all levels were involved in the recruitment process. In addition to this, every potential candidate did an on the job experience. This really helped candidates to decide whether the job was in fact for them. More importantly it gave a say to the staff whether or not the candidate would fit with the culture.

5) Run assessment centres:

Another great way to really assess for attitude is by running assessment centre days that bring in your current staff as part of the recruitment process. The 'desert island' exercise (where the group are asked to chose from a list of essential items if they were stranded on a desert island) demonstrates well how people work in groups, how they negotiate, what their thought process is, how they put their point of view across and how they interact with each other.

6) Always be on the look out:

Always be on the look out for people with the right attitude in the marketplace. When you see someone who clearly embodies the qualities you want on your team, give them your card and invite them to get in touch. As any good manager knows, that extremely attentive waiter or patient sales person could be your next great team member.

7) Referral scheme:

Introduce a referral scheme to staff. Make it as generous as you can whether in terms of money or days off. If you pay a recruitment agency then think how much it costs per hire and offer a large percentage of that to your staff.

Your staff know who will make a good employee and who will fit with the team.

8) Observe applicants when they think no one is watching:

Observing how they behave when they think no one is watching will show you a candidate's true colours. Ask your receptionist to make a note of how people behave when they come in.

How did the applicant treat your receptionist? Did he/she strike up conversation with other applicants in the waiting room? Did he/she eat alone at lunch or did he/she introduce himself to a table of strangers?

What the candidate says and does outside of the manager's view can give you a glimpse into their true personality. This may differ from how they present in an interview. Use these clues to help judge if the applicant will really be a good fit with your culture.

Hiring for attitude is about building a distinctive workplace culture and company brand that, unlike skill sets, can't easily be copied in the market. It's what gives Pret a Manger, Southwest Airlines and Ritz-Carlton their unique character and competitive advantage.

Follow the lead of these legendary firms as you look to recruit great candidates. Don't just hire for skill; hire for attitude. It makes all the difference.

39

PROCESS IMPROVEMENT AND REDESIGN

Why review your processes?

Reviewing your processes can be a significant determinant of the quality of the customer experience, which in turn can drive great differences in margin.

It is really important that managers are constantly aware of the processes that exist within their business that may be helping or hindering the customer experience. Many retailers spend thousands of pounds on marketing campaigns that drive new footfall into their stores only to disappoint those customers because of processes that are working against staff helping to engage with these new customers.

A classic example is the planning of lunch or coffee breaks. If breaks are planned over the busy trade periods, it's only logical that the business will be left with insufficient front-line manpower at the time it needs it most. When a customer needs help but cannot find a member of staff to help, invariably they will leave the store disappointed and quite possibly without making a purchase. This could just be the start of the damage as they are unlikely to revisit and secondly they will tell others – we all do!

Another common example is when head office request for certain tasks to be carried out. Many front-line teams will believe that any request from head office needs to be done immediately and will prioritise these tasks over helping their customers. Now I am not saying that we should ignore head offices across the country but we must make sure that they do everything they can to ensure that front-line staff are free to engage with their customers when they are in your stores. There are many times within the trading window that there are few customers entering your business. It is not rocket science, to ensure that the head office requests are directed towards this time.

Deliveries are another example: if not scheduled in a commercial way they can distract front-line teams and this in turn has a negative impact on the customer experience. Not only is the timing of the delivery important but so is the prioritisation of putting out stock once a delivery has arrived. How many times have we as customers had to fight our way around stores because the shop floor is full of boxes or trolleys? Now any retailer knows if stock is in the stockroom rather than on the shopfloor it cannot be sold, but there is a difference between ensuring new lines are put out immediately and the back up stock is prioritised for when the store is less full of customers.

It is important therefore that managers are equipped with the skills and confidence to examine their own internal processes critically, and then to identify and redesign any bottlenecks to customer excellence.

So how can you determine which processes to address?

Ideally, let your customers decide. If we have listened to what our customers are saying we should be in good shape to determine which processes are either working or not working. Focus on the processes that directly affect the customer experience.

Process review does not need to be complicated. It can instead follow the simple stages as outlined below:

1) Identify and analyse process

Identifying a process that is working against giving a great customer experience is the starting point. Your customers will tell you which these are if you ask them.

2) Map current process

Once identified, map the current process out on paper in stages from end to end. This should be done with the people who are closest to the process. Begin at high level and then decompose to the next sub level, until you have enough detail to understand how it really works and can identify the issues.

3) Identify issues

Next identify the issues that are preventing you giving a great customer experience. These could be duplication, slow decision making, not done right first time etc. Think about what is critical to your customers experience and view the issue through this lens.

4) Redesign process

Imagine how the process could work better avoiding the bottlenecks.

Question whether you actually need this process. Is it being done by the right person with the right skills or could/should someone else do it?

Think through how it could be done differently, adding in stages that may make it more effective or taking out stages that are unnecessary based on your previous analysis. Be aware of and take into account other areas of the business or indeed other businesses that do it better.

Now remap the new process.

5) Implement new process

Put the new process to the test.

6) Review new process

Review the new process. If it works, communicate to the rest of the team. It would be really valuable to get customers to give you feedback on it. It should then be reinforced with observations from front-line teams. If it requires further process redesign due to other issues, repeat from stage four to stage six.

40

COMMITMENT

"Never doubt the power of a small group of committed people to change the world. That's about the only way it has ever happened in the past."
Margaret Mead

Exercise

What does the word 'commitment' mean to you?

-
-
-
-
-
-

(Suggested answers: Makes it happen, Action, Marriage, Children etc.)

Lots of people make out they are committed and even say they are committed but then just get bogged down in the everyday stuff.

What differentiates someone who is truly committed from someone who says that they are but really is not? Commitment is not a word that should be thrown around a room from one person to another like a frisbee! It is however, something for which you are prepared to be on the hook for. It is something that you are prepared to take total responsibility for. So, my question to you all is, "What are you all prepared to take total responsibility for?"

It's now time to put together a commitment plan as to how you personally are going to keep your team fired up and ready to go so that they engage effectively with your customers.

I recommend you come up with just four or five things that you believe will really make a difference to you and your teams. Things that that you are prepared to be accountable for. Things that you are prepared to be on the hook for.

Revisit these on a regular basis to check whether you have achieved them, to check that they are still relevant and to check that you are on track with them.

My commitments

1.

2.

3.

4.

5.

41

FIRE UP YOUR ORGANISATION

You can bring Energize to your organisation by contacting them at:

info@energizelearning.com

If you would like to contact Steven direct, please do so at:

steve@energizelearning.com
07946 398831.

Alternatively, you can contact our offices at:

Energize Learning Ltd
Oak House
15 Hodford Road
London NW11 8NL
Telephone 0208 731 9464

We very much look forward to hearing from you.

APPENDICES

APPENDIX 1

CASE STUDIES

1. Major UK department store

Business Challenge

A major department store on Regent Street London was failing to provide a high level of service to its customers. Results from a mystery shop programme showed that customers were not being greeted or approached and when customers attempted to connect with staff, the response from them was not consistently helpful. In addition to this, low morale existed amongst the team and staff turnover was high.

Desired Outcomes

The owners wanted to build value in anticipation of selling the business and so the Energize programme was designed to support the delivery of the following outcomes.

Key metrics

- Retail sales to increase by 6% year on year.
- Mystery shop scores to increase by 10%.
- Labour turnover to reduce by 15%.
- Customers to have a better and more consistent shopping experience.
- Create a service culture that is supported by positive attitude and a defined set of behaviours.

- An exceptional customer and colleague experience.
- Managers and staff to feel more valued and confident.

How Energize Helped

Energize developed a programme that addressed the store's needs. Following a comprehensive diagnosis, they developed a modular campaign that ensured the teams in store digested the learning in bite size chunks.

"The modular approach has paid considerable dividends in our performance" according to the Director of Human Resources, "Sales are up 9% on last year and mystery shop scores a staggering 25% up on pre development visits."

Energize also developed a leadership programme that equipped all managers with the confidence and skills to coach their teams and sustain the behaviours introduced within the programme in the medium term.

"The managers left their sessions confident in being able to role model the behaviours and coach their staff on the behaviours on the front-line" added the Director of Human Resources.

"The Spiral of Positivity is a great tool to enable staff across the whole of retail, to understand that they choose how they respond to whatever happens to them during the day and it is no surprise that it has become the signature for the programme," commented the Retail Operations Director.

Value Delivered

There was a significant change in performance and atmosphere.

Key metrics

- Sales up 9% on last year (target 6%).
- Mystery shop scores up 25% (target 10%).
- Staff turnover down 24% on last year (target 15%).

Customers and staff experience

- Fewer complaints and more compliments.
- More humour, smiles and laughter.
- An overall improvement in attitude has been apparent throughout the store.
- More collaborative work across departments.
- Less blame and more problem solving.
- Many influential members of the team have become exceptional role models.

Client reviews

The Retail Operations Director commented, "We have created substantial value through increased sales and a large reduction in staff turnover. This is supported by consistent increases in mystery shopper scores."

The Director of Human Resources added, "One of the most satisfying results is that the change is lasting. Sustainability was one of my key priorities and now all the teams use phrases and tools from the Energize programme in their daily conversation. It's not just part of a customer service campaign – it's part of our culture. We would recommend Energize to any organisation that truly wishes to help its front-line teams engage positively with their customers."

2. The Curo Group 2014 (housing association)

Summary

The Curo Group, the Bath and Bristol-based housing association, has increased customer satisfaction by 46%, improved staff engagement by 61% and taken steps to become an employer of choice after implementing a company-wide development programme to put its customers first.

Energize Learning designed and delivered the 'Customer Experience' programme for Curo's 450 colleagues, from the frontline to the chief executive. By developing customer-centric attitudes and behaviours, the modular programme has brought tangible benefits, helping Curo to further differentiate its offering as it expands its commercial activities.

Driving a customer-centric culture at Curo Group

In 2012, four housing organisations, owning 12,000 homes around Bath and Bristol, came together to become a single brand and one of the largest social landlords outside of London. The new company took the name Curo (meaning 'I care' in Latin) and set about creating a five-year strategic plan outlining its vision, its values and its six business priorities. It then commenced a radical programme of change which involved the restructuring of teams and processes and the refurbishment of its premises.

"Our number one priority from the outset has been to create a renowned customer service culture," said Donna Baddeley, Curo Group's Executive Director of Transformation and Business Improvement. "It's part of building our brand and strengthening our offer to the market. To provide the best possible experience for the people who live in our properties or use our services, we have to put the customer at the heart of everything we do. We decided to introduce a company-wide customer experience programme to help everyone in the business develop the attitudes and behaviours that would enable us to achieve this aim."

From a tender process that attracted 30 submissions, Curo selected Energize Learning to design and deliver the customer experience programme.

"We were looking for a tailored development solution that would instil a 'way of being' with our customers," said Donna Baddeley. "Energize was the unanimous choice of our selection panel because they understood what we were trying to achieve and they recommended an ideal programme that would enable us to clarify exactly what we meant by customer service and what we expect from our colleagues."

Diagnostic stage

To understand the interactions between Curo's colleagues and customers, Energize's lead facilitator attended home visits with its tradesmen and studied its call centre and inter-departmental operations. Focus groups of residents and colleagues were held to identify and discuss key service challenges and a 'visioning' workshop on excellent customer service was run for the executive team.

"Energize got under the skin of our operation to understand not only the challenges that our colleagues face in their day-to-day roles but also the context in which they're working," said Donna Baddeley. "This was really useful as it meant they could support concepts in the programme with relevant examples from the business."

Modular approach

Energize delivered two separate modules for all of Curo's 450 colleagues. The first was run for mixed cohorts of colleagues, which brought people together from different parts of the business. It began with a short video that Energize had produced, showing external and internal customers talking about how they like to be treated. The session examined the essence of great customer service and highlighted the importance of attitude, listening skills, questioning, taking ownership and understanding customer emotions. Colleagues were asked to consider personal changes that they could make in their work practices, to bring the customer service vision to life.

The second module was delivered for colleagues in their teams and focused on resolving difficult customer situations and how teams could work together more productively to meet the needs of internal and external customers. Each team made their own commitments about how they could work more collaboratively to benefit their customers.

Energize ran separate sessions for Curo's 70 managers, outlining their responsibility as role models and how they could use coaching to encourage and reinforce the right behaviour. A 'train the trainer' session was also delivered, to enable Curo to run the programme itself for new colleagues as they join. To help sustain the learning, individual colleagues were asked to volunteer to become internal champions of the approach. Energize then ran a session on how these champions could promote good practice internally and ensure that individuals and teams lived the commitments they had made to improve customer service across the organisation.

"It's been an excellent programme and all aspects of it were focused on our needs, highly engaging and expertly facilitated," said Donna Baddeley. "We can definitely see tangible benefits throughout the business. People are more motivated, they're more focused on meeting the needs of customers, they're choosing their attitude, encouraging others to be positive and using the concepts and terminology from the programme. It's had a significant impact."

Success factors

As well as working in partnership with Energize, Curo has taken other steps to ensure the success of the programme.

"Having the executive team fully behind the programme has been massively important in showing colleagues that we're genuinely committed to customer care," said Donna Baddeley. "Also, we've run the programme with rigour and discipline after establishing a project board to oversee the implementation. We've reinforced the key messages from the programme internally via posters and visual reminders and we're also introducing a monthly recognition scheme for colleagues to promote and embed the desired behaviours."

Sustaining the transformation

Curo commissions independent surveys of its customers and it uses an indicator called 'net promoter score', to gauge customer satisfaction and the loyalty of its customer relationships. "Our customer net promoter score has increased by 46% and that's a direct correlation of the improved service we're now delivering," said Donna Baddeley. "Customers are also saying we're living our values more. On top of that, our staff net promoter score has increased by 61%. All of these improvements can be traced back to the Energize programme."

As Curo expands its commercial activities, Donna Baddeley says the benefits of the programme could have far-reaching implications.

"If our colleagues are unfailingly courteous and polite, and they go the extra mile for customers, that will clearly drive customer loyalty," she said. "Plus, if we're seen as positive and progressive, we'll become an employer of choice and that will help us to attract and retain great people. Because of our commercial activities, we increasingly need to appeal to private customers, as we're committed to shared ownership and we're creating a new house building division and introducing holiday lets. Consequently, our reputation in the market is now even more important. If we can differentiate ourselves in terms of being ethical, offering value for money and delivering excellent service, that will help us achieve our ambitious growth plans. The Energize programme and the changes we've made in every part of our business have placed us firmly on the road to reach that goal."

About the Curo Group:

Curo provides affordable homes and high quality care and support services across the West of England. www.curo-group.co.uk.

3. Enfield Primary Care Trust

Business Challenge

Enfield PCT clearly recognised the importance of customer service to their organisation as well as the challenges of actually getting service right on the front-line, where the patient experience is generated.

Enfield's goal was to improve patient experience – both the level and consistency – across a dispersed and varied organisation, especially in an environment where there had been, and would continue to be, high levels of change.

The Enfield leadership knew the types of behaviours they were looking to see, but were equally clear that an improvement in key metrics was also required, not only to demonstrate the value of the programme, but also to reinforce and sustain success.

The target areas for improvement were mystery patient scores, complaints and a significant improvement in staff survey – both response rate and scores on key questions.

How Energize Helped

Energize began by consulting with key members of the team across the many sites to construct a vision of the ideal behaviours to support a consistent, high quality patient experience.

They then developed a programme which was participative and engaging for all staff called "Living our customer first".

"It was a very positive programme. It gave our staff an opportunity to step into the shoes of our patients and think about what we are doing and how we are doing it," says Cathy St John, Provider Division Performance Manager.

Energize then trained a group of champions to cascade the programme across sites and functions – this was a mix of clinical and non-clinical personnel. "The train the trainer sessions gave me the skills and confidence to roll the programme out to my own and other teams," says Liz Barry, Modern Matron, Magnolia Unit.

In addition to this, a managers' support programme was

implemented to ensure that momentum was sustained. "A very useful and easy to use coaching model which I know will help to keep the training alive," says Marion Andrews Service Manager, District Nursing.

The Energize Customer Service Programme was designed to help support a transformation across the Provider Division of the Primary Care Trust to:

- Create an environment where staff treat patients as they would like to be treated.
- Effect a change in attitudes and behaviours that would significantly improve the service culture.
- Introduce specific, appropriate skills to enable staff to deliver excellent customer service.

More specifically Energize facilitated a Vision Workshop to define the desired outcomes:

- Patients feeling warmth, that they are being heard, cared for and have their fears alleviated.
- Hearing "Let me find another appointment that suits you", and offers of help.
- Feeling a calmer environment.
- People working together as a team – colleagues treating each other with respect.
- Staff welcoming patients with a smile and eye contact.
- Staff going the extra mile, feeling proud, relaxed, stress free.
- Staff and patients smiling.

"What I liked about the Energize visioning process was that it enabled us to define clearly the key behaviours we needed our staff to be demonstrating with our patients and each other," commented Julia Brown – Chief Operating Officer.

Value Delivered

"We always felt that we were looking to achieve a change in culture and especially a change in attitude and behaviour. We also needed to show success across key metrics."

Enfield commissioned a mystery shopper company Retail Maxim to run a mystery reporting programme. From the pre-programme baseline score there was an overall improvement of 14% and now across all areas Enfield are in the 90th percentile.

"These great results show we reinforced those departments that were doing well and motivated others to improve their interaction with the patients," says Cathy St John.

In addition, compliments have increased and formal and informal complaints have dropped, "complaints are being dealt with earlier before escalating."

On the staff side there has been a significant improvement in atmosphere and performance. "Teams are working together in a more collaborative way. Many individuals are showing far more confidence, initiative and ownership leading to a faster resolution of issues. 'You are the difference' was a great way of bringing teams together," says Julia Brown.

A further significant sign of improvement in staff engagement was that completion of the staff survey turned around from 42% to 64%.

Julia Brown commented in closing: "There is no doubt that 'Living our customer first' by Energize has made a huge contribution to our overall transformation."

4. Sodexo UK Finance Shared Service Centre

Business Challenge

The Shared Service Centre was not providing a sufficiently high level of service to its customers: suppliers, clients, employees and the finance functions of the various Sodexo UK entities. There was a culture where many interactions were confrontational, where email created a defensive, one way style of communication and where morale was low.

This had a number of implications: the emergence of shadow finance functions involving duplication of activity and costs; unwillingness to transfer additional services and limited joint working together on process reengineering, all resulting in lost opportunities to add value, reduce costs and working capital or improve billing and cash flow.

The Energize Customer Service Programme was designed to support a transformation in the Centre to:

- Help individuals and teams understand and believe they are in control of how they work and the quality of service they both provide and receive.
- Create an environment where centre staff treat customers as they would like to be treated.
- Effect a change in attitudes and behaviours that will significantly change the service culture.
- Introduce specific, appropriate skills to enable staff to deliver excellent customer service.

How Energize Helped

At speed, Energize developed a programme that exactly addressed Sodexo's needs and was according to Lisa Crawley, Shared Service Director, "unlike any other programme we have seen. It was highly participative, engaging, funny, short and amazingly effective." The programme immediately generated a buzz so that, after the first day, getting attendance of subsequent groups was easy. It was also non-threatening which made the world of difference to the front-line, often quite junior team members.

Although there were a wide number of issues to deal with, the programme built on strengths rather than start from scratch. Indeed, the Energize team really took "time to understand us, our teams and our challenges" observed Lisa. A key part of the programme was to ensure that the various parts of the Transformation Programme were complimentary and not competing.

Value Delivered

There has been a significant change of atmosphere and performance. Tangible changes include:

- Faster resolution of issues. Less wasted time.
- More initiative and ownership, less dependency.
- More collaborative work across functions with the business.
- Less blame and more problem solving.
- Fewer complaints and more compliments.
- Less email traffic and more conversations.
- More humour, smiles and laughing.
- At an individual level many influential – and not necessarily the most senior – members of the team have become exceptional role models.
- Some less helpful staff have improved significantly their attitude and performance.
- The overall improvement in attitude has also enabled other changes to be introduced more easily.

"The improvements have created substantial value through greater accuracy, greater insight, greater speed and all of these with less resources," commented Aidan Connolly, Sodexo UK CEO. "But the real prize is that we have moved most of the UK Finance Operations into the Shared Service Centre. Previously as each process moved from each area, it was a challenge – now the businesses are queuing up to move. The value created from this has been very significant.

"A further major benefit was enabling the Finance team to move from being a processing factory to a business partner. Putting a value on this is very difficult but very large."

"For me," added Lisa, "one of the most satisfying results is that we were able to keep it going. Sustainability was one of my key priorities."

5. Medtronic Pain Therapies

Third Annual Congress of the World Institute of Pain, Barcelona, September 2004

Introduction

Energize were asked to adapt their signature programme "Living our customer first" for a multi-national team from Medtronic, one of the world's leading medical technology companies. Medtronic were exhibiting at an international medical conference in Barcelona and, although they had considerable previous conference and exhibition experience, they recognised the importance of maximising the number of new leads, and were keen to invest in training for the team working at the conference. The objectives of the training were:

- To demonstrate tried and tested tools and techniques for engaging prospective customers as they passed by or approached the conference stand.
- To focus on the importance of attitude as the key to maintaining motivation whilst manning the stand throughout the conference.
- To create a team atmosphere among all personnel who were not all familiar with one another, being based in various different European offices.
- To ensure that sufficient information was collected from prospective customers to enable effective follow-up action to be taken after the conference.

Preparation and delivery of the programme

As part of the process of adapting and customising "Living our customer first" for Medtronic, Energize had numerous discussions with people at various levels within the company, in order to gain a full understanding of the team's performance and perception of previous conferences and to learn about Medtronic's products and services as well as its culture. The results of these discussions shaped the way in which Energize designed the programme for the congress, and ensured that it fully reflected specific Medtronic terminology and nuances. Time was also spent on securing the buy-in and commitment of Medtronic's senior managers, to ensure that they were fully aware of the content and had a chance to contribute their input, as well as appreciating their role in encouraging and supporting the programme.

The programme was delivered on-site to the 20 Medtronic delegates shortly before the start of the conference, following a general team briefing. This minimised time spent away from the conference and enabled the team immediately to put these new skills and capabilities into practice on the stand.

There were two parts to the programme: a two hour core interactive training session to provide the team with the skills, knowledge and confidence to enable staff to engage naturally in conversation with customers, followed by "Life on the front-line", where the members of the Energize team joined and worked alongside Medtronic staff and management on the stand itself, providing hands-on coaching to ensure that the team had fully mastered the skills and techniques taught in the core session.

Outcome and results

300 new contacts were made, which equated to a 600% increase in the number achieved compared with the previous conference.

The core session was well received, with lots of positive feedback from the participants. At the end of the core session, each participant was asked to complete and submit a commitment plan, and encouraged to set themselves personal and team targets of numbers of contact leads they would obtain from visitors to the stand.

A rota had already been drawn up, with a minimum of 4 people manning the stand at all times during the conference. A team leader was designated for each time slot. Following the core session, it was agreed that the team leader would hold a short briefing and debriefing session with their team members when starting and finishing their session on the exhibition stand, in order to set targets, review performance and keep the team motivated and enthusiastic.

The 'Life on the front-line' session proved to be an enormous success. The Energize team members spent two hours on the stand with Medtronic personnel immediately after the core session, and a further three hours with the teams manning the stand the following morning. The Energize team showed how the techniques taught worked in practice, and helped to engage conference delegates coming on to or passing by the stand in conversation.

The impact of the programme was powerful. Certain team members who had initially appeared somewhat sceptical of the simplicity of the techniques coached, found to their amazement and delight that they really did work! Prospective customers felt comfortable with being engaged in this way, and the team found that they could effortlessly engage them in conversation, using the tools and props available on the stand. As the numbers of contact lead forms collected increased, so did the confidence and enthusiasm of the team on the stand.

Records of the numbers of leads collected by each team during their session on the stand were collated and a chart was drawn up to engender a sense of competition among the teams manning the stand.

"You can really see the difference as a result of the Energize programme: leads collected were up 600% on the previous event. The power of the training lay in its simplistic approach but it simply did the job as the figures show!" comments Marta Gehring, Marketing Director, Medtronic Pain Therapies.

APPENDIX 2

LIST OF QUOTATIONS

"There is little difference in people, but that little difference makes a big difference. The little difference is attitude. The big difference is whether it is positive or negative."

Clement Stone

"No one can make me feel inferior without my consent."

Eleanor Roosevelt

"Determine that the thing shall be done, and then we shall find the way."

Abraham Lincoln

"If you think you can or you think you cannot you are right."

Henry Ford

"If you always do what you have always done, you will always get what you have always got."

Henry Ford

"You cannot discover new oceans unless you have the courage to lose sight of the shore."

Andre Gide

"Feel the fear and do it anyway."

Susan Jeffers

"Never, never, never, give up."

Sir Winston Churchill

"Let us be grateful to people who make us happy; they are the charming gardeners who make our souls blossom."

Marcel Proust

"Seek first to understand, then be understood."

Stephen Covey

"Things that matter most should never be at the mercy of things that matter least."

Stephen Covey

"Give a man a fish and you feed him for a day, teach him to fish and you feed him for life!"

Ancient Chinese proverb

"The one who listens does the most work, not the one who speaks."

Stephen Covey

"The key to listening is with the eyes and the heart."

Stephen Covey

"What gets measured gets done."

Tom Peters

"What gets measured get improved."

Robin Sharma

"Never doubt the power of a small group of committed people to change the world. That's about the only way it has ever happened in the past."

Margaret Mead

APPENDIX 3

CLIENTS THAT HAVE EXPERIENCED OUR PROGRAMMES

Retail

Aspinal
Adams Childrenswear
Ann Summers
Bare Escentuals
Berwin Retail
B&Q
Box Fresh
Bed and Bath works
Chatwins Bakery
Crème de la Mere
Crew Clothing
Christy
Debenhams
Dorothy Perkins
Dunelm
Emmerson property group
Fat Face
French Connection
Gant
Hugo Boss
Highland Distillery
The Iron Bed Company
Jaeger
Jenkins Bakey
La Coste
Levi Strauss
Liberty

Lombok
Marks and Spencer
Moss Bros
Mothercare
Newlook
Orvis
Past Times
Pringle
Paper chase
Petit Bateau
Pia Jewellery
Playtex
Sainsbury
Selfridges
Smith News – Connect Group
Superdrug
Tesco
The Co-operative Society
Toys R Us
TM Lewin
TK Max
Value Retail
Vivienne Westwood
Viyella
White Stuff
W H Smith
World Pearl Company

Leisure

Ascot
The Premier League
Glasgow Rangers
Vue Cinema
Sodexo
Skrill
Prestige

Public Sector

The Curo Group – Housing
Audit Commission

Healthcare

Great Ormond Street Hospital
Croydon PCT
Enfield PCT
Haringey PCT
Dolland & Aitchison
Rayner Opticians
Medtronic
Next Pharma

Education

The London Business School
Explore Learning
Sylvan Learning

Finance

Barclays Bank
Brooks MacDonald
Royal Bank of Scotland
Reich Insurance